THE ENCYCLOPEDIA OF PSYCHOACTIVE DRUGS

SERIES 1

SERIES 2

BAD
TRIPS

GENERAL EDITOR
Professor Solomon H. Snyder, M.D.

*Distinguished Service Professor of
Neuroscience, Pharmacology, and Psychiatry at
The Johns Hopkins University School of Medicine*

•

ASSOCIATE EDITOR
Professor Barry L. Jacobs, Ph.D.

*Program in Neuroscience, Department of Psychology,
Princeton University*

•

SENIOR EDITORIAL CONSULTANT
Joann Rodgers

*Deputy Director, Office of Public Affairs at
The Johns Hopkins Medical Institutions*

THE ENCYCLOPEDIA OF
PSYCHOACTIVE DRUGS
SERIES 2
BAD
TRIPS

MARK S. MILLER

CHELSEA HOUSE PUBLISHERS
NEW YORK • NEW HAVEN • PHILADELPHIA

EDITOR-IN-CHIEF: Nancy Toff
EXECUTIVE EDITOR: Remmel T. Nunn
MANAGING EDITOR: Karyn Gullen Browne
COPY CHIEF: Juliann Barbato
PICTURE EDITOR: Adrian Allen
ART DIRECTOR: Giannella Garrett
MANUFACTURING MANAGER: Gerald Levine

Staff for BAD TRIPS:

SENIOR EDITOR: Jane Larkin Crain
ASSOCIATE EDITOR: Paula Edelson
ASSISTANT EDITOR: Michele A. Merens
EDITORIAL ASSISTANT: Laura-Ann Dolce
COPYEDITOR: Ellen Scordato
ASSOCIATE PICTURE EDITOR: Juliette Dickstein
PICTURE RESEARCHER: Debra P. Hershkowitz
DESIGNER: Victoria Tomaselli
PRODUCTION COORDINATOR: Laura McCormick
COVER ILLUSTRATION: Betsy Scheld

CREATIVE DIRECTOR: Harold Steinberg

Extract from "The Eden Express" by Mark Vonnegut © 1975. Reprinted by permission of Knox Burger Associates Ltd.

Extract from "High Priest" by Timothy Leary © 1968. Reprinted by permission of Timothy Leary.

3 5 7 9 8 6 4 2
Library of Congress Cataloging-in-Publication Data

Miller, Mark S. (Mark Shepherd), 1952–
Bad trips
  (The Encyclopedia of psychoactive drugs. Series 2)
  Bibliography: p.
  Includes index.
  1. Psychotropic drugs—Physiological effect—Juvenile literature.
2. Hallucinogenic drugs—Physiological effect—Juvenile literature. 3. Substance abuse—Juvenile literature. [1. Hallucinogenic drugs. 2. Drugs. 3. Drug abuse]
I. Title. II. Series.
RM315.M48 1988   615'.788   87-14605

ISBN 1-55546-218-9

CONTENTS

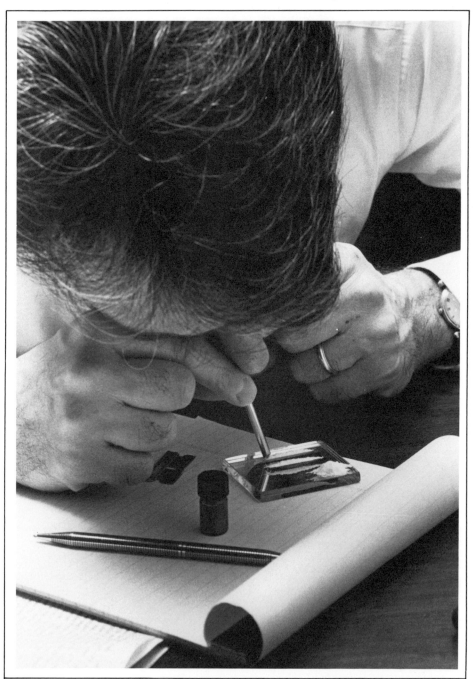

This user may be looking for a "quick lift" by snorting cocaine, but, like most psychoactive drugs, cocaine has a number of negative side effects that outweigh any high it induces.

In the Mainstream
of American Life

One of the legacies of the social upheaval of the 1960s is that psychoactive drugs have become part of the mainstream of American life. Schools, homes, and communities cannot be "drug proofed." There is a demand for drugs — and the supply is plentiful. Social norms have changed and drugs are not only available—they are everywhere.

But where efforts to curtail the supply of drugs and outlaw their use have had tragically limited effects on demand, it may be that education has begun to stem the rising tide of drug abuse among young people and adults alike.

Over the past 25 years, as drugs have become an increasingly routine facet of contemporary life, a great many teenagers have adopted the notion that drug taking was somehow a right or a privilege or a necessity. They have done so, however, without understanding the consequences of drug use during the crucial years of adolescence.

The teenage years are few in the total life cycle, but critical in the maturation process. During these years adolescents face the difficult tasks of discovering their identity, clarifying their sexual roles, asserting their independence, learning to cope with authority, and searching for goals that will give their lives meaning.

Drugs rob adolescents of precious time, stamina, and health. They interrupt critical learning processes, sometimes forever. Teenagers who use drugs are likely to withdraw increasingly into themselves, to "cop out" at just the time when they most need to reach out and experience the world.

Young people often mix drugs and alcohol in social situations. Alcohol heightens the effects of other mind-altering substances; its interaction with certain depressants can be lethal.

Fortunately, as a recent Gallup poll shows, young people are beginning to realize this, too. They themselves label drugs their most important problem. In the last few years, moreover, the climate of tolerance and ignorance surrounding drugs has been changing.

Adolescents as well as adults are becoming aware of mounting evidence that every race, ethnic group, and class is vulnerable to drug dependency.

Recent publicity about the cost and failure of drug rehabilitation efforts; dangerous drug use among pilots, air traffic controllers, star athletes, and Hollywood celebrities; and drug-related accidents, suicides, and violent crime have focused the public's attention on the need to wage an all-out war on drug abuse before it seriously undermines the fabric of society itself.

The anti-drug message is getting stronger and there is evidence that the message is beginning to get through to adults and teenagers alike.

The Encyclopedia of Psychoactive Drugs hopes to play a part in the national campaign now underway to educate young people about drugs. Series 1 provides clear and comprehensive discussions of common psychoactive substances, outlines their psychological and physiological effects on the mind and body, explains how they "hook" the user, and separates fact from myth in the complex issue of drug abuse.

Whereas Series 1 focuses on specific drugs, such as nicotine or cocaine, Series 2 confronts a broad range of both social and physiological phenomena. Each volume addresses the ramifications of drug use and abuse on some aspect of human experience: social, familial, cultural, historical, and physical. Separate volumes explore questions about the effects of drugs on brain chemistry and unborn children; the use and abuse of painkillers; the relationship between drugs and sexual behavior, sports, and the arts; drugs and disease; the role of drugs in history; and the sophisticated drugs now being developed in the laboratory that will profoundly change the future.

Each book in the series is fully illustrated and is tailored to the needs and interests of young readers. The more adolescents know about drugs and their role in society, the less likely they are to misuse them.

Joann Rodgers
Senior Editorial Consultant

Aldous Huxley chronicled his frightening experiences with mescaline in his book The Doors of Perception. *The drug's extreme hallucinogenic effects made him feel as if his personality were "disintegrating."*

INTRODUCTION

The Gift of Wizardry
Use and Abuse

JACK H. MENDELSON, M.D.
NANCY K. MELLO, Ph.D.
Alcohol and Drug Abuse Research Center
Harvard Medical School—McLean Hospital

Dorothy to the Wizard:

"I think you are a very bad man," said Dorothy.
"Oh no, my dear; I'm really a very good man; but I'm a very bad Wizard."
—from THE WIZARD OF OZ

Man is endowed with the gift of wizardry, a talent for discovery and invention. The discovery and invention of substances that change the way we feel and behave are among man's special accomplishments, and, like so many other products of our wizardry, these substances have the capacity to harm as well as to help. Psychoactive drugs can cause profound changes in the chemistry of the brain and other vital organs, and although their legitimate use can relieve pain and cure disease, their abuse leads in a tragic number of cases to destruction.

Consider alcohol — available to all and yet regarded with intense ambivalence from biblical times to the present day. The use of alcoholic beverages dates back to our earliest ancestors. Alcohol use and misuse became associated with the worship of gods and demons. One of the most powerful Greek gods was Dionysus, lord of fruitfulness and god of wine. The Romans adopted Dionysus but changed his name to Bacchus. Festivals and holidays associated with Bacchus celebrated the harvest and the origins of life. Time has blurred the images of the Bacchanalian festival, but the theme of drunkenness as a major part of celebration has survived the pagan gods and remains a familiar part of modern society. The term "Bacchanalian Festival" conveys a more appealing image than "drunken orgy" or "pot party," but whatever the label, drinking alcohol is a form of drug use that results in addiction for millions.

The fact that many millions of other people can use alcohol in moderation does not mitigate the toll this drug takes on society as a whole. According to reliable estimates, one out of every ten Americans develops a serious alcohol-related problem sometime in his or her lifetime. In addition, automobile accidents caused by drunken drivers claim the lives of tens of thousands every year. Many of the victims are gifted young people, just starting out in adult life. Hospital emergency rooms abound with patients seeking help for alcohol-related injuries.

Who is to blame? Can we blame the many manufacturers who produce such an amazing variety of alcoholic beverages? Should we blame the educators who fail to explain the perils of intoxication, or so exaggerate the dangers of drinking that no one could possibly believe them? Are friends to blame — those peers who urge others to "drink more and faster," or the macho types who stress the importance of being able to "hold your liquor"? Casting blame, however, is hardly constructive, and pointing the finger is a fruitless way to deal with the problem. Alcoholism and drug abuse have few culprits but many victims. Accountability begins with each of us, every time we choose to use or misuse an intoxicating substance.

It is ironic that some of man's earliest medicines, derived from natural plant products, are used today to poison and to intoxicate. Relief from pain and suffering is one of society's many continuing goals. Over 3,000 years ago, the Therapeutic Papyrus of Thebes, one of our earliest written records, gave instructions for the use of opium in the treatment of pain. Opium, in the form of its major derivative, morphine, and similar compounds, such as heroin, have also been used by many to induce changes in mood and feeling. Another example of man's misuse of a natural substance is the coca leaf, which for centuries was used by the Indians of Peru to reduce fatigue and hunger. Its modern derivative, cocaine, has important medical use as a local anesthetic. Unfortunately, its increasing abuse in the 1980s clearly has reached epidemic proportions.

The purpose of this series is to explore in depth the psychological and behavioral effects that psychoactive drugs have on the individual, and also, to investigate the ways in which drug use influences the legal, economic, cultural, and even moral aspects of societies. The information presented here (and in other books in this series) is based on many clinical and laboratory studies and other observations by people from diverse walks of life.

Over the centuries, novelists, poets, and dramatists have provided us with many insights into the sometimes seductive but ultimately problematic aspects of alcohol and drug use. Physicians, lawyers, biologists, psychologists, and social scientists have contributed to a better understanding of the causes and consequences of using these substances. The authors in this series have attempted to gather and condense all the latest information about drug use and abuse. They have also described the sometimes wide gaps in our knowledge and have suggested some new ways to answer many difficult questions.

One such question, for example, is how do alcohol and drug problems get started? And what is the best way to treat them when they do? Not too many years ago, alcoholics and drug abusers were regarded as evil, immoral, or both. It is now recognized that these persons suffer from very complicated diseases involving deep psychological and social problems. To understand how the disease begins and progresses, it is necessary to understand the nature of the substance, the behavior of addicts, and the characteristics of the society or culture in which they live.

Although many of the social environments we live in are very similar, some of the most subtle differences can strongly influence our thinking and behavior. Where we live, go to school and work, whom we discuss things with — all influence our opinions about drug use and misuse. Yet we also share certain commonly accepted beliefs that outweigh any differences in our attitudes. The authors in this series have tried to identify and discuss the central, most crucial issues concerning drug use and misuse.

Despite the increasing sophistication of the chemical substances we create in the laboratory, we have a long way to go in our efforts to make these powerful drugs work for us rather than against us.

The volumes in this series address a wide range of timely questions. What influence has drug use had on the arts? Why do so many of today's celebrities and star athletes use drugs, and what is being done to solve this problem? What is the relationship between drugs and crime? What is the physiological basis for the power drugs can hold over us? These are but a few of the issues explored in this far-ranging series.

Educating people about the dangers of drugs can go a long way towards minimizing the desperate consequences of substance abuse for individuals and society as a whole. Luckily, human beings have the resources to solve even the most serious problems that beset them, once they make the commitment to do so. As one keen and sensitive observer, Dr. Lewis Thomas, has said,

> There is nothing at all absurd about the human condition. We matter. It seems to me a good guess, hazarded by a good many people who have thought about it, that we may be engaged in the formation of something like a mind for the life of this planet. If this is so, we are still at the most primitive stage, still fumbling with language and thinking, but infinitely capacitated for the future. Looked at this way, it is remarkable that we've come as far as we have in so short a period, really no time at all as geologists measure time. We are the newest, youngest, and the brightest thing around.

BAD
TRIPS

High on LSD and seemingly oblivious to his surroundings, this user walks barefoot along a rooftop. Hallucinogens distort reality and can sometimes lead to self-destructive behavior.

CHAPTER 1

BAD TRIPS—THEN AND NOW

It began slowly — a realization that something was wrong. I was lying on the bed watching a talk show on television. I had just smoked a couple of joints with my girl friend. Good marijuana, it had a mellowing effect. It produced a sense of calm, everything floating quietly. No fast rushes or disturbances. It was like any other time I'd smoked dope. Mellow.

But then it began.

At first it was just a sense of uneasiness. I felt uncomfortable. The room felt a little distorted, and I was having trouble concentrating. I had trouble focusing on the television screen. Then I found it difficult to focus on the show. I was having trouble understanding the talk show host. He was just finishing up an interview, but that's all I could figure out. I was having difficulty understanding the language — it was as if he were talking another language entirely, one I couldn't understand.

I looked around the room, trying to get my bearings, but I couldn't focus on anything for any length of time. My eyes were particularly sensitive to light, and the small lamp on the bedside table seemed to burn with an intensity I'd never seen before. My eyes were beginning to hurt. They were darting from object to object — a poster on the wall, a photograph on the dresser, the television. And still the television blared on, and I still couldn't understand it.

I tried to concentrate on the talk show host. He was talking away. The earlier interview was over. He was about

19

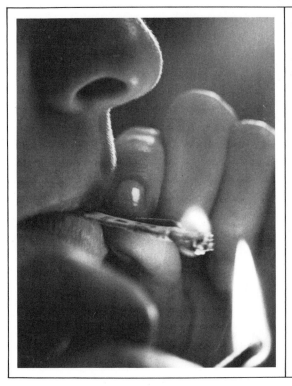

Recent research has proven that marijuana can be psychologically addictive, leads to personality disorders, and does more damage to the lungs than cigarettes do.

to introduce another guest, and I could feel my anxiety increase. Suddenly, with no reason to explain it, I felt I was the next scheduled guest on the show. I felt I was being sucked into the television show and that I would be the next guest to face the talk show host. I felt I would — at any moment — be sitting across from him, unable to understand anything he was saying. And he would be asking me question after question, smiling at me, waiting for an answer.

My mouth became like cotton, and I could hear my heart throbbing. I couldn't let it happen. What would I say? What did I know? I would look like a fool. I couldn't be dragged into the television. I had to get away, to run.

I jumped off the bed and ran into the bathroom. I could hear my girl friend shouting at me from the other room, wanting to know what was wrong. I couldn't answer. By now I was petrified, and — worse still — I believed I would remain scared for the rest of my life. I felt the world was an awful place to be and that there was no escaping it. I was painfully aware of my existence, and I felt so alone.

I was stooped over the toilet trying to throw up — trying to get rid of whatever it was that I had taken. I felt for sure

*that I was tripping [under the influence of an hallucino-
gen]. Somehow I had taken LSD instead of grass. Somehow
I had gotten some acid [LSD] mixed up in my system. I had
tripped on acid once before, and it had been a bad experience. I thought I must be having a flashback [a reoccur-
rence of an earlier drug experience]. I was tripping again.*

*I ran to the telephone and called the friend who had
turned me on to the sticks of marijuana. I dialed the number. After a few moments a woman answered. It was my
friend's sister.*

"What's in this dope?" I asked.

"It's good, isn't it?" she said.

I could tell from her voice that she was stoned.

*"What's wrong with it?" I asked again. "I feel like I'm
tripping."*

*"It's just strong dope," she said. "It's Mexican. Don't
worry."*

*She hung up and I was on my own. For the rest of the
night I stayed awake. I was scared more than I'd ever been.
I spent the night praying and trying to vomit whatever it
was I had ingested. Finally I fell asleep.*

*The next day I was still anxious. I went through the
day fearful that the feelings of the night before would return. My girl friend was fine, but I was still scared.*

*For months I carried around the fear of that night,
worried that I would flash on the event and find myself
tripping again. Finally I went to a doctor who prescribed
some tranquilizers for me, and ultimately I went into ther-
apy. In time, I came to see that I had been under immense
pressure in the weeks before the incident. But still, my reaction had been a drug-induced experience.*

*Some friends and experts I've told about this experience
seem to think the marijuana I smoked was treated with
something — maybe a little angel dust, or some other hallucinogen. Trip weed, some have called it. Others think I
was simply reacting to stress in my life, which was intensified while under the influence of marijuana. Still others
think I must have latched onto some very potent grass,
maybe from Southeast Asia or some other area where marijuana has a much stronger content of THC [the psychoactive ingredient of marijuana].*

*I never found out for sure, and for years it haunted
me. Was it the drug or was it me?*

Bad trips, bummers, come-downs, flashbacks, freaking out, tripping out. These are all terms that mean the same thing: adverse drug reaction. As in the case above, they are unpredictable events. The young man who smoked what he thought was marijuana will never know for sure what it was that prompted such a strong reaction. He had smoked marijuana many times, and he firmly thought no harm would come to him from occasional drug use. But it did — just as it has for many people.

Turn On, Tune In, and Drop Out

When Timothy Leary advised a generation to "turn on, tune in and drop out," there were plenty of people who thought the former Harvard psychologist turned guru was right on target. It was the late 1960s, and according to the lyrics of a popular song from *Hair*, the Broadway musical that supposedly — if some critics were to be believed — defined a generation, "the youth of America [was] on LSD."

During the late 1960s one-time Harvard professor Timothy Leary, notorious for his heavy experimentation with LSD, urged young people throughout America to "turn on, tune in and drop out."

It was an interesting time. There was a sense that nothing like this generation had ever existed before — and never would again. For one thing, its members had discovered so much — including the mystical properties of chemically induced experiences. This was a new age. The age of freedom — freedom from convention, from limitations, from authority. It manifested itself in the music, the social amenities, and what was dubbed by the press as "The Counterculture" and —on some occasions—"The Drug Culture."

Drugs — and particularly powerful hallucinogens, such as LSD (lysergic acid diethylamide) — were being touted by some of the most popular celebrities as vehicles to use on the road to self- discovery. The Beatles sang about "Lucy in the Sky with Diamonds," and many people secretly smiled when they listened to the lyrics; however much the rock group denied it, audiences were sure that the first letters of "Lucy," "sky," and "diamonds" were a code that spelled out LSD when strung together. There was a sense that drugs and their mystical effects had been discovered for the first time. For many, it was a time of mystery, of initiation, of discovery. It also turned out to be — for many — a time of tragic consequences.

Good and Bad Trips

For all the mystery and excitement, for all the trappings of a generation supposedly experiencing great epiphanies, the drug culture was also on its way to far more painful realizations. Many soon came to understand or discover that just as there were "good trips," there were "bad trips," also known as "freak-outs" and "bummers." A generation of "druggies," or "freaks," or "heads," as some called themselves, soon realized that the pleasures of drug-induced mystical experiences were often outweighed by dangerous side effects.

By the time Tom Wolfe wrote *The Electric Kool Aid Acid Test* in 1969, chronicling the adventures of novelist Ken Kesey and his friends as they rode across country in an old school bus, the bad trip was rapidly becoming a fixture of the counterculture. And just as Kesey and his friends sustained casualties on the road during their long trip, so, too, did they sustain casualties when they used LSD — or "acid," as it was popularly known — to fuel their long inner journey.

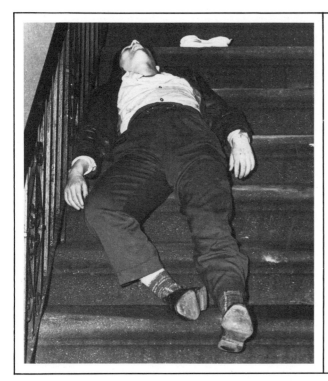

A man lies dead, the victim of a heroin overdose. The downside of even casual drug use is the "bad trip," an unexpected adverse reaction to a drug that can result in psychotic behavior, frightening flashbacks, or even death.

Because of Wolfe and other popular writers, America read about getting lost along the way, heard about the "bummer," and came upon the less glamorous side of drugs.

In drug circles, the news was already known. Caution became a common practice. News of bad acid or bad hog, (a name for PCP, or phenylcyclidine, also known as angel dust), for example, would filter through the counterculture, passed from one person to the next through such neighborhoods as San Francisco's Haight-Ashbury — the mecca of the "turned-on generation" during the middle to late 1960s. To deal with the problem, people sought out certain types of LSD and other drugs and avoided certain others.

Soon, certain sorts of LSD and other drugs went by a host of "brand" names. The name hog, for PCP, came from the drug's commercial use as an animal tranquilizer. Peace Pills — another name used for PCP in the late 1960s — has no direct link to any particular drug effect. Names given to other drugs reflected the method of administration. Strains of LSD — white flatbacks, for example — were arbitrarily named by the chemists who manufactured them or the people who took them. Still others, such as sunshine or purple haze, supposedly reflected what one experienced or saw while under their influence. And some strains were named after their manufacturers, such as the various types of Owsley acid — named after Augustus Owsley Stanley III, one of the premier LSD manufacturers, who reportedly never indulged in LSD himself.

Like commercial products, certain brands of drugs gained sponsors. Owsley acid, for example, was prized by Kesey and the rock group the Grateful Dead. But for all its sponsors, LSD has always been an unpredictable drug. Although certain brands developed good reputations and others became known as dangerous, no one could ever guarantee the effects of any type. What was "good acid" for one person might land another in the nearest emergency room.

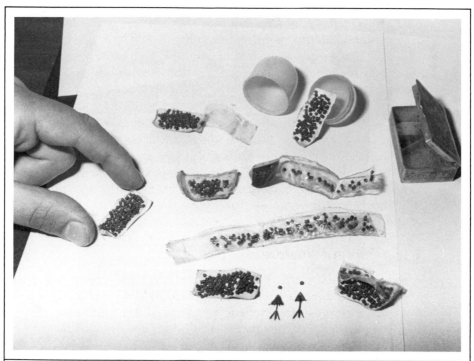

Police confiscated this drug cache, which contained 1,000 doses of LSD, in 1977. After a brief period of eclipse, LSD use among young Americans is once again on the rise.

In time, the "psychedelic stores" and "head shops" (named for *potheads* and *acidheads*), where street people and hippies congregated and bought beads, posters, and drug paraphernalia, were joined by what rapidly became another fixture of the counterculture: the street clinic. In addition to treating standard ailments, the clinics found that much of their business on any given day was from people who had overdosed on drugs or who — in popular lingo — were having "bum trips" or were "freaking out."

Recognizing the Dangers

During the 1960s, news of bad drug experiences was as familiar as beads, flowers, and rock concerts. Despite the availability of literature documenting past drug abuse and the dangers of bad trips, the harmful effects of drug use came as a surprise to many within the counterculture. Warnings in the 1950s about marijuana (some movies, for example, depicted musicians "gone bad" because they smoked marijuana and became addicted) were often ignored, for few believed what they had seen — and with good reason. There was plenty of misinformation that suggested all drugs led to addiction of some sort.

Consequently, many in the new drug culture of the 1960s went to the opposite extreme and chose to believe that all drugs could be taken without harm and that films produced earlier about the danger of drugs were little more than paranoid "establishment" propaganda. Despite these denials of the potential damage posed by drug use, the reality of bad drug experiences — and, in some cases, life-threatening drug experiences—was still unavoidable.

A Trip Through History

Many people believe that drug abuse and the use of hallucinogens are a fairly recent phenomenon. History, however, indicates otherwise. Psychedelic plants played a significant role in the cultures of the Old World. Opium was long a drug of choice in the eastern hemisphere, as was cannabis (marijuana) and, of course, alcohol. Drug use in general dates back to the earliest days of our species. Scientists have found evidence that plants with medicinal properties were buried in the graves of Stone Age people.

Taken in 1925, this stylized photograph captures a group of opium smokers in New York City's Chinatown. Such opium dens were common in the early part of the 20th century.

There also are graphic examples of drug abuse and its consequences throughout history. Frightening experiences fill historical accounts of religious rites of passage, bacchanals, and orgies. Accounts of addiction pepper the pages of history. From the opium dens of ancient China to those of San Francisco in the last century, from accounts of hashish use by Indian holy men to opium use by Persian mystics, from descriptions of alcohol abuse in ancient Greece and Rome to reports of narcotics abuse by 19th-century British poets seeking inspiration, the history of drug abuse is an old one. Equally old are the reports of its unfortunate consequences.

Anxiety, depression, paranoia, and even psychosis are among the list of mental disturbances produced by a wide variety of drugs, ranging from powerful hallucinogens, such as those found in peyote and other plants, to minor intoxicants and stimulants, such as wine and nicotine. In the religious rites of several Central American Indian tribes, where the use of hallucinogens is common, there are stories of those who became lost between the worlds of reality and spirit, never to return mentally. The Indians are but one example of a people who are fully familiar with the dangers associated with using powerful hallucinogens. When the Spanish encountered *datura inoxia* (a powerful hallucinogen known as *toloatzin* or *toloache* to the Aztecs) during their conquest of Central America in the 15th and 16th centuries, they called it *hierbo del diablo*—the devil's herb.

Much of the language used to describe drug experiences today can be traced back to earlier times. The term "trip" dates back to traditional South American Indian concepts, such as those held by the Cashinahua tribe of Peru, who use hallucinogens on religious vision quests. Tribe members speak of their experiences as journeys, and as some of their journeys can be bad, they will wish each other well before a drug experience, telling each other in their native tongue to "have a good trip."

Language of the Modern Age

It was not until the 1960s that drugs became firmly established in modern culture, and a whole new language — sometimes borrowing from the old — came into being. The term *trip*, for example, once only a noun, has become a verb as well — full of action and power. People trip, or — in bad situations — "trip out," describe their experiences as "tripping," and refer to particularly potent forms of drugs as "trip" substances. "Trip weed," for instance, refers to very potent forms of marijuana or marijuana that has been treated with some hallucinogenic substance such as LSD or PCP.

Many of the terms used to describe drugs and the drug experience also reflect the alienation of the age and are violent in nature. For example, people are said to "crash" after a drug experience, and the term aptly describes the depression that often accompanies withdrawal from the influence of LSD, amphetamines, or other drugs. (Street wisdom has it that the crash — or "bring down," as it is also called — is harder for some "heads" than others. Because those who sniff glue ["glue heads"] or abuse amphetamines ["speed freaks"] often experience depression and physical discomfort that includes headaches and chills from withdrawal, many try to stay high for as long as possible.) And those who take drugs are often referred to — or, in many cases, refer to themselves — as "freaks," "junkies," "dopers," and by an assortment of other names that suggest alienation from society.

A Reliance on Drugs

Many have speculated about the increase in drug use in the last half of this century. There are no definitive answers for the question of why so many have come to look to drugs for relief, entertainment, mystical experience or any number of other experiences, but there are clues.

Ours is the first age in which people have been able to solve countless physical and mental problems with drugs.

After a drug experience, many people "crash" and fall into a depression that may last for hours or even days. This aftereffect is particularly brutalizing when it follows use of a stimulant such as cocaine.

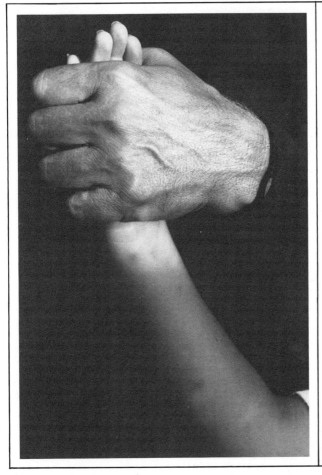

No drug can cure grief, frustration, or disappointment. Individuals should draw on their own inner resources and the support of family and friends when confronted with periods of great stress or adversity.

Diseases have been wiped out through widespread vaccination, others are prevented because of inoculations, and still others are controlled to such a great degree that millions of people who once would have been institutionalized for psychotic conditions can live relatively normal lives thanks to psychoactive medication.

But there is a danger to watch for.

In the last half of the century — and especially in recent years — drug production has become a big business. As researchers have identified ever-more-effective drugs, people have come to depend more on these chemicals and to look for answers to their problems in the bottom of pharmacists' vials. Ours has become a society of drug takers, dependent on everything from common aspirin to tranquilizers to alcohol — a trend that only recently has begun to change as physicians and other educators have begun talking extensively about the dangers inherent in drug dependence.

Unfortunately, many people still think that drugs are the answer to a host of problems that should not be treated with chemicals in the first place. Not only are illnesses and debilitating conditions cause for physicians' prescriptions in their minds, but the human condition, as well, seems ripe for treatment with chemicals and compounds. What once took some imagination or a little willpower to control now seems to be the legitimate province of drugs. People too often have turned to drugs to control virtually everything in their lives. There is the sense in some quarters that anything can be cured with the right drug — grief, frustration, disappointment, ordinary anxiety, perhaps even boredom.

Plenty of people have tried to reach for that idyllic world. What few have realized — at least not right away — is that there is a price to pay.

Experts agree that people with psychological problems are particularly susceptible to the adverse effects of powerful mind-altering drugs.

CHAPTER 2

BAD TRIPS: HOW THEY HAPPEN

Why is it that some drugs have such beneficial effects while others have the power to unleash very dangerous results? What is it that makes a powerful hallucinogen, such as LSD, spell disaster for one person and yet leave another person virtually untouched? Why are drugs such an unknown quantity?

These are all worthwhile questions. There are answers to some of them. Others are still being debated and studied. We know a great deal about how drugs work, but we have yet to answer all the questions regarding why drugs affect people differently. Even those who advocate drug use as a form of enlightenment have been at a loss to explain definitively why the hallucinogens they promote as vehicles to self-discovery can affect people differently — why, for example, one person can take a certain strain of LSD and have a pleasurable experience, and another person who takes the same dosage at the same time and in the same place ends up in the midst of a hideous nightmare, perhaps with irreversible effects.

Psychological and Physical Reactions

When it comes to different responses to drugs, much of the answer appears to be a question of psychological makeup. Psychiatrists and psychologists on all sides of the drug debate have agreed that people with psychological and emotional difficulties are more susceptible to the adverse effects of potent mind-altering drugs. In some cases, for example, people with deep-seated, unresolved emotional conflicts are brought to the brink of their ability to cope — or lose their ability altogether — when under the influence of a powerful hallucinogen. In many cases, the hallucinogen may bring problems to the surface before a person is prepared to face the conflicts. Also, the drug often magnifies those conflicts.

But whatever the contributing factors, it is important to understand how drugs act on the body.

A great many misconceptions influence our thinking about drug use. In general, society looks to drugs to treat a myriad of afflictions. There often is, however, very little comprehension of how drugs work. Television, for example, treats us to a host of simplistic descriptions. Headaches come in a few essential varieties — those depicted by hammers beating

Some psychoactive drugs can leave habitual users feeling profoundly isolated and estranged from friends and family.

away at the inside of some poor unfortunate's skull, those that are represented by flashing red lights, or those that are shown as flames of tension. However advertisers choose to depict pain, the suggested answer is almost invariably the same: Within minutes of taking a pill, the problem will be gone and the world will be filled once again with smiling, satisfied people.

The process, of course, is much more difficult and complex. Somehow, in order to obtain relief from pain or any other drug-induced change, the drug must get from the external world to the appropriate site in the body where it can take effect. That may sound simple, but quite a number of factors are involved. First, the drug must be absorbed into the bloodstream. Then it must be distributed throughout the body by the circulating blood, take effect, and, finally, be broken down into an inactive compound and excreted.

In the case of mind-altering drugs, the process is indeed complicated.

Drugs and the Brain

The brain is composed of two different kinds of cells. Glial cells, which make up 85% of the brain, are actually supporting cells, guiding the brain's development and helping to remove waste products. The remaining 15% is made up mostly of cells known as neurons. These cells, in turn, consist of the cell body (which contains the nucleus of the cell), short limblike structures called dendrites extending from the cell body, and a longer, threadlike projection called an axon. In effect, axons and dendrites are the brain's wiring system. Action, behavior, and brain activity depend on axons and dendrites because all the electrical impulses required for the brain to work must first travel down the axon, cross a tiny gap (synapse) between nerve endings, and then travel to the adjacent neuronal cell via the dendrite.

Once electrical impulses traveling down the axon reach the nerve ending, they trigger the release of chemicals that cross the synapse between the nerve endings of adjacent neuronal cells, allowing communications within the brain. The chemicals are called neurotransmitters, and they affect certain portions of the brain known as receptors. Once a neurotransmitter affects a specific receptor, it either slows

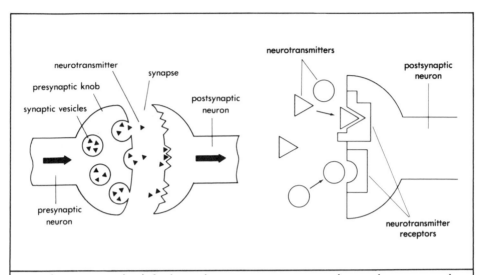

The drawing on the left shows how one neuron signals another across the synapse between them by emitting neurotransmitters. The illustration on the right shows how each kind of neurotransmitter fits only one kind of receptor on the target neuron.

or speeds the rate of brain communication depending on what kind of neurotransmitter it is. But, in any case, it triggers a new electrical impulse in the receiving brain cell, continuing the process and allowing neurons to communicate with each other.

Scientists have shown that neurotransmitters — constructed from precursor chemicals already in the body — act on receptors in much the same way that a key fits in a lock. Consequently, certain neurotransmitters are perfectly suited to affect certain neurons. For example, certain specific chemicals have a great affinity for those receptor sites belonging to cells that control respiration or sleep. Others seem tailor-made to act on those receptors that control pleasure and pain.

Recently, scientists have concluded that at least 50 distinct neurotransmitters are responsible for relaying communications in the brain. Meanwhile, scientists at the National Institutes of Health, Johns Hopkins University, and other prestigious medical centers have in recent years been able to map the brain's molecules, identifying — among other things — those neurotransmitters and receptors that they think control pain, pleasure, and addiction, as well as the receptors that supposedly control body movement. Their research has not only led to a greater understanding of how the brain works but has enabled physicians to move a step closer to unlocking the mysteries of a host of major psychiatric disorders.

When psychoactive drugs enter the brain, they act either as neurotransmitters attracted to certain brain receptors, or they inhibit neurotransmitters from reaching receptors. In either case they affect brain chemistry and consequently produce reactions. Morphine, for example, mimics the enkephalins (also known as endorphins). Naturally occurring opiatelike substances, enkephalins are neurotransmitters that fit into the opiate receptors in the brain, and by doing so, they alleviate pain. They also appear to encourage sleep and slow down breathing. Scientists think morphine acts like enkephalins by similarly affecting the brain's opiate receptors and producing analogous results.

Mapping the Brain

Because all other psychoactive drugs act in somewhat the same fashion, researchers have been trying to identify links between specific drugs and receptor sites in the brain that the drugs affect. Using positron emission tomography (PET) scanners to track radioactive elements that stick to the surface of certain receptors, scientists have been able to map certain types of brain activities. After a patient is injected with radioactive tracer molecules, the PET scanner charts the distribution of the tracers and identifies where specific receptors are in the brain. (The tracer emits a tiny amount of radioactivity — not enough to harm the patient, but just enough to be detected by the PET scanner.) Once it identifies specific receptor sites, the scanner notes what effect certain drugs and other chemicals have on those areas of the brain.

In the hope that physicians will eventually have a new tool to detect and treat major mental illnesses, scientists are currently using this mapping technique to conduct studies that will determine the effect of certain drugs on the brain. One study in particular involves people who have been addicted to narcotics and are being treated at certain U.S. Veterans Administration hospitals in the Washington, D.C. area and elsewhere. Other studies involve the effect of various forms of anesthesia and of drugs used to treat schizophrenia and other mental illnesses.

The Good, the Bad, and the Very Bad

So what determines whether the use of a particular drug will prove pleasant or unpleasant?

No drug has one single effect. In fact, all drugs — whether therapeutic or not — have some toxic effect. Even aspirin, which is taken by many people at the first symptom of a cold or headache, is actually a very powerful analgesic (pain reliever) that can have such unpleasant effects as stomach discomfort. And some antibiotics, which are essential in the treatment of infections, can produce nausea, sensitivity to sunlight, and even depression. Those discomforting effects are called side effects for good reason. Because a drug is designed to produce a specific result, or *main* effect, anything that is considered an unwanted result is known as a *side* effect.

In some cases, one person's side effect is another person's main effect. For example, although morphine is a strong and effective pain reliever, it also has a number of side effects — including constipation. And while constipation may be an unpleasant side effect to someone who is using the drug for pain relief, it may be the main effect for someone who is being treated for severe diarrhea.

The same is often true with drug abuse. The "high" or intoxicating effects certain drugs produce may be considered unpleasant side effects for certain people; for others, the high is the desired effect. Amphetamines are a good example. Some people take them for weight control and reluctantly put up with the nervous jitters that the drugs give them. The amphetamine abuser, however, cares little about weight control and instead searches for the nervous "rush" (so called because of the "rush" of adrenaline the drug produces). For the amphetamine abuser, the drug's usual *side* effect becomes the *main* effect.

When a drug produces the effect it is supposed to, we think of it as a beneficial — sometimes pleasant — experience. When it comes to recreational drug use — or drug abuse — the desired effect is usually stimulation, pleasurable experience, or some other desirable result. Consequently, much of what people call pleasant or unpleasant experiences — good or bad trips—depends on very personal interpretations.

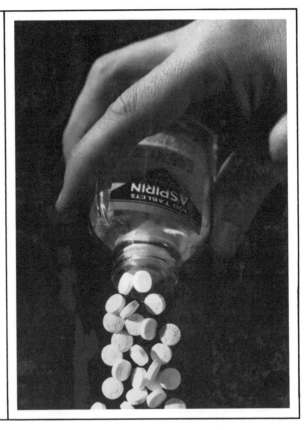

Some people suffer from stomach disorders as a side effect of using aspirin. Fortunately, aspirin substitutes are available to help such individuals cope with minor pains.

But even in this rather subjective area, there are certain agreed-upon definitions. Traditionally, the drug culture has quite simply characterized certain drug reactions as bummers or bad trips when the negative aspects have outweighed the pleasurable and enlightening ones. That has often been the case when dealing with powerful hallucinogens.

LSD, for example, often produces unpleasant experiences. People who are under the influence of LSD or some other hallucinogen often drift into the negative end of the emotional spectrum. Side effects include confusion, acute panic, dissociative reactions, a reliving of earlier traumas, and, in some instances, acute—or temporary—psychosis.

Even supposedly good experiences can include pain, anxiety, and terror. Consider the following description of an LSD experience by none other than Timothy Leary, one of the counterculture's strongest advocates of LSD use:

The Timothy Leary game was suspended and the needle point of consciousness was free to move into one of thirteen billion nerve cells or down any one of a billion genetic-code networks.

... First the dial swung to the sensory.... Then the dial swung to the olfactory sensations. The room was filled with spaghetti tangles of smell tapes, and dog-like, I sorted through them. I could see each distinctive fume of scent....

Then consciousness buried itself in tissue memories. A rapid newsreel sequence of my life. Early childhood picture albums. Model A Fords. Cotton candy at the beach....

Sudden revelations into the workings of oxygen monopoly. In the year 1888, British scientists ... discover that the oxygen supply of the earth is failing. [They] secretly bottle remaining vapors of air and hide it. Air is replaced by synthetic gas which possesses no life or consciousness, keeps people alive as plastic doll robots....

The rest of the human race is doomed to three-D-treadmill plastic repetition. Trapped...

Science fiction horror. Hell! I wanted to shriek and run from the room for help. How to get back to life. Center. Pray. Love.

I sank back into delightful tissue recollections— muscle memories. I could feel each muscle in my shoulders and legs swelling, pulsing with power. Felt the hair growing on my limbs and the elongated dog-wolf foot-pad legs loping and ... then death. Heavy, cold immobility creeping up my body. Oh God. Now be careful how you lie. Your posture will be frozen into a mountain marble landscape statue.... So this is death. Good-bye to animal mobility.... Now the elderly elemental mineral consciousness takes over. Had you forgotten? Rocks are aware....

For millenia I lay in geological trance. Forests grew on my flanks, rains came, continental ecstasies.... I opened my eyes. I was in heaven. Illumination. Every object in the room was a radiant structure of atomic-god-particles. Radiating. Matter did not exist. There was just this million-matrix lattice-web of energies.... Everything hooked up in a cosmic dance. Fragile. Indestructible....

And then the incredible shattering discovery. Consciousness controlled it all.

> I was staggered by the implication. All creation
> lay in front of me. I could live every life that had ever
> been lived, think every thought that had ever been
> thought. An endless variety of ecstatic experience
> spiraled out around me. I had taken the God-step.

Although Leary saw his experience as essentially illuminating, he also admitted the horror. Few drug experiences — even among those of the drug culture's "high priests" (Leary called himself one of the culture's leaders) — have been without frightening and potentially dangerous adverse reactions.

The unpleasant experience can indeed end up being a very long, bad trip. Physicians have noted a significant number of prolonged disturbances resulting from LSD use, including distortions in perceptions of time and space, changes in body image, and residual fear or depression resulting from the original bad trip.

All of the above, as in the case of any drug action, depends on chemicals that find their way to the brain receptors mentioned earlier. Why then do some people experience pleasure and others experience pain? The answer is as simple as noting the different reactions people have to dosage and as complex as speculating on the role brain abnormalities and psychological makeup play in drug reactions. Dosage and psychological factors aside, those who have severe reactions to LSD and many other drugs may have abnormalities in the number of neuroreceptors that those drugs affect. Although little is known regarding how LSD and some other hallucinogens create their effect, researchers think the drugs are in some way related to serotonin, a neurotransmitter that affects brain communication and the peripheral nervous system.

Research suggests that LSD, dimethyltryptamine (DMT), psilocybin, and some other hallucinogens mimic serotonin, which is used by the raphe cells (neurons at the top of the spinal cord) to send messages to centers in higher brain regions. Those centers, in turn, help regulate emotions and vision, and the hallucinogens have the effect of slowing the raphe cells' activity, which causes hyperactivity in the higher brain regions. (Research also suggests that some types of mental illness may be associated with abnormalities in communication between serotonin neurons.)

How Much Depends on Environment

Aside from specific questions regarding brain chemistry, there is also the question of the setting. In other words, how much do a person's surroundings have to do with whether he or she has a good or bad drug experience?

From chronic abusers to first-time experimenters, the consensus is that the setting plays a significant role in the way many drugs affect people. This is especially true with hallucinogens — everything from LSD to marijuana — which make people extremely sensitive to external stimulation.

Psychiatrists, psychologists, and other experts have long observed that emotional response is influenced by environment. Setting has also been a major concern within the drug culture. Proponents of LSD and other hallucinogens in the 1960s and 1970s often talked about just the right setting for "tripping." In fact, a common practice for first-time LSD users was to use an experienced "guide" — one who had taken LSD a number of times before — to help him or her through the first trip. Drug users also talked about "contact highs," which were drug-free highs induced simply by being immersed in a suggestive setting, complete with psychedelic lights, incense, acid rock (a style of music that extolled the use of hallucinogens) and the presence of people who were actually high.

From Use to Abuse

If you take too much of any drug, most likely you will have some sort of adverse reaction. Amphetamines, for example, have long been used to control appetite. When taken under the close supervision of a physician, they can prove helpful to severely obese people who are unable to lose weight without some initial help in controlling their diet. If abused, amphetamine use can easily lead to addiction, psychosis, and even death. The same can be said of such opiates as morphine, an important pain reliever that can also lead to addiction as easily as any opiate available on the street and, if taken in sufficient quantities, can result in death.

With such hallucinogens as psilocybin and psilocin — two psychedelic agents found in at least 15 species of mushrooms and often referred to on the street as "magic mushrooms" — adverse reactions are very much a result of dose. Used in a number of religious rites among Indian tribes in Central and South America, the drugs are approximately 200 times less potent than LSD — which produces effects closely resembling those of psilocybin and psilocin — and can sometimes produce mild, pleasant experiences when taken in low doses. When taken in larger amounts, they produce perceptual alterations, occasional hallucinations, and serious consequences. (Even in low doses, these drugs can be highly unpredictable and dangerous, especially for people with a history of emotional problems.)

The same can be said for almost any powerful drug — the list, quite frankly, is endless. It is often a very subtle step

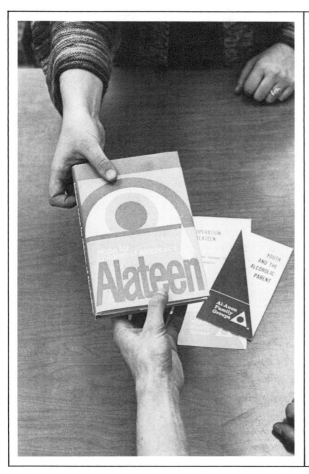

Studies indicate that the children of alcoholics often become alcoholics themselves. Such groups as Alateen have been formed to help these young people cope with their alcoholic parents and their own inclination to use the drug.

A person who indulges too often in social drinking can be an alcoholic without knowing it. The line between alcohol use and abuse is a fine one, and such warning signs as blackouts should be taken seriously.

from drug use to drug abuse — and it is often very difficult to tell who will eventually take that step.

The progression from alcohol use to abuse is probably the most familiar of all. It is also very difficult to say definitely what will and will not lead to alcoholism. There are, of course, the classic warning signs of alcoholism — dependence on the drug, blackouts, and frequent intoxication, to name a few — but it is not easy to pinpoint who will eventually progress from social drinking to alcoholism. Whereas recent research is pointing increasingly to the conclusion that many forms of alcoholism are inherited, in some instances it is not due to a genetic predisposition at all. For example, many people who are prone to depression use alcohol as a form of self-medication; others use this drug in an equally self-defeating effort to cope with anxiety disorders. Needless to say, such self-treatment ends up becoming a major problem in itself.

The role heredity often plays in addiction raises significant questions regarding whether there are people who have addictive personalities. Although physicians have often talked about the "addictive personality," debate continues about whether there is truly a distinct personality type prone to addiction and whether that addictive personality can be inherited. In recent years, scientists have underscored earlier studies suggesting genetic factors in addiction. Their recent research suggests that chemical abnormalities in certain people may indeed make them susceptible to addiction.

With alcoholism, for example, numerous studies strongly indicate that it is an inherited disease for many people. Far too often, what begins as social drinking leads to alcoholism in people who are susceptible. One study — conducted as a collaborative Danish-American investigation during the early 1970s — found that sons of alcoholics are four times more likely to become alcoholics themselves. Other recent studies — which also indicate genetic factors at work — suggest that alcoholics do not have the biological protection against alcohol that nonalcoholics have. Most people, it seems, get some type of warning as they become intoxicated. Alcoholics, however, don't appear to get the message because of enzymatic differences.

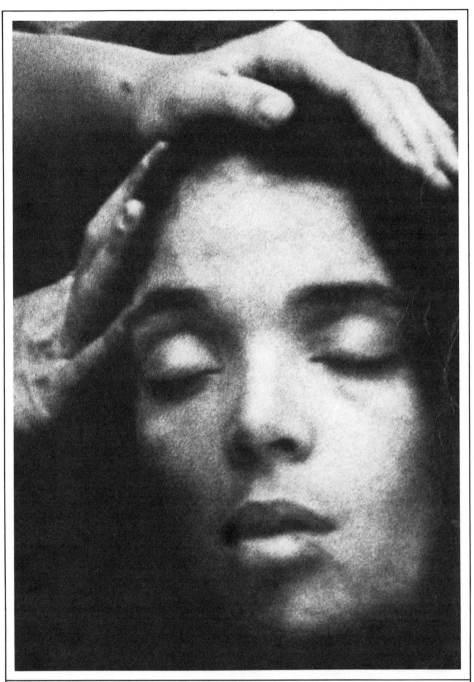

Irreversible psychosis is one potential consequence of a "bad" trip. Although such organic brain damage is rare, medical experts do not discount it as a possible hazard of drug use.

CHAPTER 3

BAD TRIPS AND MENTAL DISORDERS

Most people who decide to use drugs for recreational purposes rarely think of unpleasant consequences. Instead, they think of the pleasure, the excitement, and — in some cases — the status that comes with their new view of drugs. But powerful drugs, such as the hallucinogens and amphetamines mentioned in earlier chapters, can produce a wide assortment of dangerous side effects that cause tragic — sometimes deadly—results such as irreversible psychosis.

Drugs and Mental Illness

Mental disorders are among the most serious consequences of drug abuse. Drugs can precipitate acute and chronic psychosis, exacerbate underlying emotional problems, heighten neurotic tendencies, and cause organic brain damage. And although the more serious irreparable reactions — irreversible psychosis due to organic brain damage — are fairly rare, even the most vocal proponents of recreational drug use acknowledge the dangers. The best of trips, they admit, can include moments of high anxiety and deep depression.

But many of those who turn to drugs for enlightenment claim that drug use is no more dangerous than such sports as mountain climbing or soaring. To achieve the exhilarating moments, they say, one has to be willing to put up with pain,

Casual use of marijuana and other drugs may sometimes seem to offer an easy release from boredom or anxiety. Often, though, this type of escape only deepens psychological or spiritual malaise.

discomfort, and danger. Physicians and other experts, however, dismiss such simplistic arguments. Taking powerful drugs for recreational purposes is, they say, like ingesting strong poisons, not like participating in physically demanding sports.

As a rule, experts have divided bad trips into four distinct categories: sensory and social, somatic (having to do with physical reactions), psychological, and metaphysical (having to do with philosophical outlook). To some degree, bad trips that result in serious mental disorders touch on each of those categories. In the worst cases, drug reactions so severely affect a person's psychological makeup that there is a break with reality. The same is true when drugs affect the body to the point that brain damage occurs — as can be the case, for example, with serious amphetamine abuse.

Drugs and the Ego

By far the most common example of how drugs can precipitate emotional problems is when unresolved conflicts are brought to the surface of a person's consciousness. As a person grows, he or she builds defenses against certain conflicts. Known as ego defenses, these psychological fortifications are a person's way of protecting his or her own sense of identity. Sometimes these defenses are erected by the mind as a psychological response to painful events. Certain drugs can erode these defenses, making people vulnerable to repressed feelings and memories with which they are not prepared to deal. When they face those feelings and memories prematurely, the result can often be severe anxiety, panic attacks, and—in some cases—acute psychosis.

For the most part, these reactions disappear when the effect of the drug or drugs wears off. In other instances, however, the conflicts revealed may be so traumatic that they take on a life of their own, causing long-term neurotic — or even psychotic — reactions. In some instances, people mistake the nightmare feelings induced by their bad trips for reality.

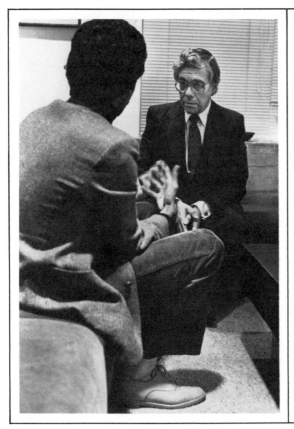

Sometimes drug trips can make a person aware of previously suppressed inner conflicts. Psychotherapy can help such an individual cope with these often troubling realizations.

Theirs are metaphysical reactions, causing them to believe they have learned something hideous and unavoidable about the very nature of life; in time their distorted perceptions can result in full-blown depressions or chronic anxiety.

The Insanity of Drugs

Among the most common examples of this type of reaction are "acute anxiety/panic reactions" or "acute paranoid reactions" to marijuana. Most marijuana smokers will attest to transient moments of paranoia and anxiety, but they are quick to add that the benefits they claim to gain from smoking are worth those moments. In some instances, however, the anxiety does not go away as the influence of marijuana wears off.

Consider the following account of one young man's experience with marijuana. For him, anxiety experienced while smoking marijuana brought out unresolved fears that lingered long after his body was clear of THC (the psychoactive ingredient in marijuana).

I'd been smoking dope for years, so I was no stranger to its effects. I'd had moments when I got all uptight, and I knew times when I got a little paranoid — you know, like when you think somebody in the room with you might be a cop and that you might get busted. But this was different.

I'd smoked a little dope, and then I really got uptight. Out of the blue, the thought struck me: "Boy, you're going to die someday." I had never been so scared in my life. What was life all about, anyway? I had always been someone who never spent very much time worrying about anything, and now I was worried to death. I couldn't sit still. I thought I'd really come unglued. I tried to talk myself down, but it was hours before I was finally able to go to sleep.

The next morning, when I woke up, I was still scared. I felt like a curtain had been drawn across my life. I felt like there was nothing to live for because we all were going to die anyway. I felt sad and scared at the same time. Then I thought for sure that I was losing my mind — maybe, I thought — I'd already lost it. There was nothing I could do, was there? I was so uptight, and there seemed to be no coming down.

When the feelings didn't go away, I just tried to live through it. Sometimes I'd be walking down the street and would feel scared for no reason. Sometimes it would be because I was thinking about life and how I was going to die someday. That would make me depressed, and then I'd feel there was no way out of the depression, and that would make me uptight.

I really thought there was no way out of it. By now I no longer associated my feelings with marijuana. I just knew the world was bad news.

Then, one day, about a year after I'd had my first panic attack, I had a real bad one. I had started college, and was between classes when it hit. I thought I was losing my mind. Every part of my body was tight, and I could feel my head spinning. I was in the middle of town and I was afraid I'd start screaming and the police would come and take me away to a mental institution.

Instead, I went over to [the] student health [department] at the university. I told them what was going on and they sent me to a doctor across town. I told him everything, and he prescribed a tranquilizer for me. That brought me down enough to face my fears.

It took me a few years of seeing a psychologist to realize that the marijuana I'd smoked lowered my defenses enough to cause me to face a fear of death that I didn't even know I had. Maybe in time I would have faced it slowly and come to accept it, but I didn't have that choice. One day I thought it was great to be alive, and the next I only wanted to die. It took me a long time to realize again that life is worth living.

Hallucinogens and Bad Trips

The above account is certainly compelling, but the consequences of bad trips resulting from more powerful hallucinogens are far more riveting. In fact, LSD, certain other hallucinogens, such as PCP (phencyclidine), and some powerful amphetamines may be responsible for precipitating crises by mimicking certain neurotransmitters and actually causing chemical imbalances in the brain. In the case of PCP, researchers are not sure what causes the action; however, the drug can often produce acute and long-lasting psychosis

Patients are counseled in a mental hospital. The adverse effects of certain mind-altering drugs can cause symptoms that mimic those of such mental disorders as psychosis and schizophrenia.

and its effects are consequently being studied as a chemical model for psychosis. Many experts believe the imbalances most likely caused by these drugs are similar to ones they expect to find at the root of most serious mental disorders.

As we have already mentioned, drug action depends on chemicals finding their way to the brain's neuroreceptors. Certain long-term adverse reactions to LSD, mescaline, DMT, and other psychedelic drugs may be the result of a person having abnormal numbers of the neuroreceptors that those drugs affect. Researchers think LSD and some other hallucinogens are related to serotonin, a neurotransmitter that affects brain communication and emotion. They have labelled these drugs psychotomimetic drugs, which means "drugs that induce psychotic states."

Aside from the chemical similarities, there are other telling factors to consider when comparing drug experiences and mental disorders. There is, for example, a great deal of similarity in the experiences of people under the influence of certain psychedelic drugs or hallucinogens and those who have developed acute schizophrenia unrelated to drug use. Often, both types — drug-related experiences and nondrug-related ones — are rife with descriptions of cosmic awareness that are uncanny in their similarity.

In *The Eden Express* (1976), Mark Vonnegut — son of the famous novelist Kurt Vonnegut — gives a powerful description of his descent into acute schizophrenia. The similarities between Vonnegut's psychosis and such drug experiences as those described by Timothy Leary and others in earlier chapters are clear. Like Leary's drug experiences, Vonnegut's madness sounds, at times, almost metaphysical and transcendent:

> I thought about the things I had studied in religion, and about how much more of it seemed to make sense now. I had somehow touched what Jesus, Buddha, and others had been talking about. Formerly confusing phrases out of various scriptures came to me and each seemed perfectly clear. I became aware of a harmony and wholeness to life that had previously eluded me...
>
> Small tasks became incredible, intricate, and complex. It started with pruning the fruit trees. One saw cut would take forever. I was completely absorbed in the sawdust floating gently to the ground, the feel of the saw in my hand, the incredible patterns in the bark, the muscles in my arm pulling back and then pushing forward. Everything stretched infinitely in all directions....
>
> I began to wonder if I was hurting the trees and found myself apologizing. Each tree began to take on a personality. I began to wonder if any of them liked me. I became completely absorbed in looking at each tree and began to notice that they were ever so slightly luminescent, shining with a soft inner light that played around the branches. And from out of nowhere came an incredibly wrinkled, iridescent face. Starting as a small point infinitely distant, it rushed forward, becoming infinitely huge. I could see nothing else. My heart had stopped. The moment stretched forever. I tried to make the face go away but it mocked me...
>
> I was holding my life in my hands and was powerless to stop it from drifting through my fingers. I tried to look the face in the eyes and realized I had left all familiar ground.

Despite the similarities, there is little evidence to suggest that use of LSD and similar hallucinogens leads to permanent psychosis. For the most part, there is simply a strong similarity between psychosis and the psychedelic experience of LSD and similar drugs. Far more frequently, those who develop profound mental disorders after taking such drugs are people who have had a history of emotional problems.

But experts still caution people to beware. Even though the numbers are not that large, there have been enough instances of seemingly well-adjusted people becoming severely depressed, anxious, or psychotic after using hallucinogens to cause concern. The following example, reported by Dr. Harvey A. Horowitz in *Diseases of the Nervous System*, is a good case in point:

> Six months before she was hospitalized, the attractive, 18-year-old woman was described by friends as outgoing, popular, and involved in her high school's activities. She was one of the most active seniors in school and intent on achieving. Then she began to experiment with LSD, amphetamines, and marijuana, and within months she changed. Once the picture of achievement and success, she became agitated, restless, preoccupied.

> Then, after she took LSD at a graduation party, her behavior changed dramatically. She couldn't sleep, she was constantly active, incorrigibly talkative and frequently unintelligible. Her parents sought psychiatric care and she was hospitalized.

> Psychiatric evaluation showed her to be "disoriented (unable to place herself in time and space), agitated, impulsive and hyperactive, with idiosyncratic and sexually suggestive gesturing and posturing. She was sexually preoccupied, making several attempts to disrobe and make sexual advances toward male staff, cognition was grossly disturbed, the stream of ideas being irrational and incoherent."

> In addition, she suffered from delusions—most of which focused on depressing thoughts. She thought "she was pregnant, in conflict with the devil, and was going to die of cancer. Auditory and visual hallucinations were present."

> Her doctors diagnosed her condition as manic-depressive psychosis and concluded that it was probably precipitated in part by LSD.

Speed Kills

Amphetamine abuse, on the other hand, often results in severe mental disorders. Psychosis induced by methamphetamine, dextroamphetamine, and amphetamine itself, is all too well known in the medical world. On the street, the dangers are well recognized ones. In fact, a familiar saying coined in the 1960s was "Speed kills."

As in the case of LSD, there are certain strong similarities between the amphetamine experience and psychosis. The major difference is that repeated use of amphetamines, which achieve their effect by interacting with the neurotransmitters dopamine and norepinephrine, can lead to long-term psychosis and even organic brain damage; in other words, the craziness does not always go away as the drug's influence wears off.

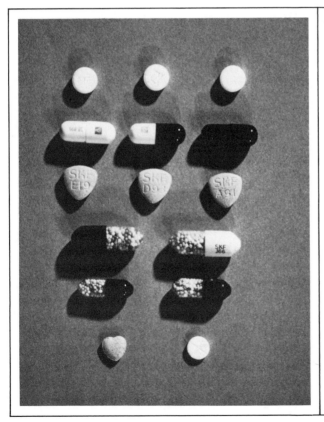

Any of these amphetamine substances can cause nervousness and irritability. Amphetamine addiction can cause long-term psychosis or brain damage.

In the following case of an 18-year-old woman, described by the Harvard Medical School professor and noted author Dr. Lester Grinspoon as suffering from amphetamine-induced psychosis, there is a striking similarity to both the LSD experience and acute schizophrenia. Compare this description with earlier ones involving LSD and the schizophrenic episode described by Vonnegut.

I felt special, destined, set apart. For the first couple of weeks I had super concentration on my homework, particularly anthropology and literature. I felt I really got inside what I read and had amazing insight. It seemed as though a genius in me was awakening.

I also got into music. It seemed fragmented and I could see sinister aspects of it.

Nature — grass, water — made me depressed to look at it. Thoughts of suicide came simultaneously with feelings of elation. I tried to commit suicide by taking aspirin, but forgot to tell the psychiatrist whom I saw a couple of days later.

When my ability to concentrate on my studies disappeared, I often found myself staring at the walls, as though I were in a trance, for maybe an hour at a time.

I suddenly became a good dancer, and felt real sexual urges for the first time in my life. I had fantasies about a man in New York whom I had fallen in love with, but with whom I had only a platonic relationship. I would come out of these reveries feeling all warm and erotic. The fantasies became uncontrollable and I began to leave behind a real-life burgeoning sex life for a deeper imaginary one. The main problem (as it had always been, only now more intensified) was that I felt separate from myself. I felt as though I were both involved in the action and observing it neutrally, like a camera. I existed on different planes. My thoughts, moods, and emotions seemed to swim by with nothing to direct them, or restrain them. I had amazing thoughts. I felt completely divided into different personalities, each one being observed by me. Sometimes the other personalities disappeared and I was totally the observer.

I often felt buoyed up to a high spiritual level by some intense mystical force.

When I tried to commit suicide the personality that was most in evidence was the one that was ridiculous, pathetic. I had often felt kind of fragmented in the past, but now, whole personalities seemed to switch on and off; I really felt like many different people. I was by turns someone who appeared to have no life of her own and no feelings, or someone completely at the mercy of fantasies, etc.

The young woman, Grinspoon points out, was in psychotherapy for several years. She eventually returned to college and graduated with honors, but she never fully recovered from her abuse of Dexedrine (a powerful amphetamine). Some years after her recovery, she took 150 mg of diethylpropion hydrochloride — normally used for appetite suppression — after a friend told her it would get her high. The results were disastrous. Three hours after taking the drug, she reverted to the acute psychosis she had experienced after taking Dexedrine and did not recover for four days.

People who are suffering psychosis caused by amphetamine abuse often experience the same symptoms as people who are schizophrenic. In fact, some amphetamine users suffering from psychosis are diagnosed as being schizophrenics before psychiatrists learn of their drug abuse. This connection has led psychiatrists to experiment with compounds that block the activity of amphetamines as possible treatments for schizophrenia.

The Most Widely Abused Drug

Alcohol is another drug that can cause mental illness. Everyone, of course, is familiar with the derelict, the skid-row bum, and the bag lady who suffer from the chronic effects of alcoholism and exhibit moments of irrationality. They are walking examples of how excessive use of alcohol over an extended period can lead to organic brain damage and — in the worst cases — irreversible psychosis. Alcohol, like many of the other drugs mentioned earlier, interferes with the production and functioning of many substances the body needs, and experts think it enhances the effect of the neurotransmitter GABA (gamma-aminobutyric acid), the body's major inhibitory neurotransmitter.

A victim of alcoholism may suffer blackouts, tremors, and memory lapses. If left untreated, this debilitating disease can cause irreparable brain damage and death.

Like many other psychoactive substances such as LSD and amphetamines, alcohol can produce temporary mental disturbances or permanent ones. Physicians generally categorize alcohol interference in brain function as *immediate* effects due to the presence of alcohol in the blood; *temporary* effects that linger even after alcohol has been eliminated from the body; and *permanent* brain damage.

Immediate effects are those a person experiences if he or she drinks too much — dizziness, lowered inhibitions, and slurred speech, for example — and are caused by alcohol's interference with the body's oxygen supply to the brain. Temporary effects are far more serious and include sleep disturbances, blackouts, hallucinations, delirium tremens (severe delirium caused by withdrawal), and seizures. In time, if a person's drinking persists, such temporary effects can become permanent because of irreparable brain damage caused by alcohol abuse.

Too Much of a Good Thing

Foreign substances that produce negative effects on the body and mind are not limited to illicit recreational drugs. In general, overdoses of almost any drug, or, for that matter, nutrient, can result in toxic levels that can produce psychosis or other serious mental disorders. The American Medical Association, for example, has long warned that certain fat-soluble vitamins — those that are stored in the body and may build up in excess amounts because the kidneys do not flush them out in the urine — can produce serious effects, including psychotic reactions. The AMA singled out vitamins A and D as being particularly dangerous when taken in excessive doses. Certainly these results attest to the fact that nutrients as well as drugs should only be taken in recommended doses.

Each of these doses of LSD, packaged on blotter paper the size of postage stamps, can send a user off on a sometimes frightening and dangerous "trip" that lasts for hours.

CHAPTER 4

HALLUCINOGENS

Overdose, insanity, death; these are the worst consequences of drug abuse. There are, however, a vast assortment of bad trips that, although unpleasant, are not quite so extreme. The bad trip can be as mild as a vague sensation of malaise and as major as respiratory failure and death. It can be the horror of a terrifying LSD-inspired hallucination, or the mild anxiety induced by too much marijuana. It can be the irreversible brain damage resulting from chronic alcoholism or the jitters from too many diet pills.

Bad trips are best discussed in terms of the major drug classifications: hallucinogens, narcotics, sedative/hypnotic compounds, and stimulants. Chapters 4 to 6 are devoted to these specific categories. Each has its own ultimate bad trip — either death or insanity — as well as lesser consequences. Suffice it to say that each group contains some very powerful drugs—drugs that should never be taken lightly.

Altering Brain Communication

Although they had been used for centuries by vastly different cultures, hallucinogens did not become major drugs of abuse until the 20th century. An important event leading to that trend occurred in 1938, when the German scientist Albert Hofmann synthesized LSD. Hofmann's discovery of the drug's effects in 1943 was accidental; he was attempting to purify lysergic acid when a trace of the substance was absorbed into his skin, causing him to experience hallucinations.

In the 1950s, several writers, including Aldous Huxley, wrote of their experiences with hallucinogens. (Huxley experimented with both LSD and mescaline, an organic hallucinogen.) By the 1960s, when LSD became the drug of choice for the counterculture, hallucinogens had become a focal point for millions of people. Although LSD was perhaps the most popular drug, others were popular as well, such as mescaline, DMT (dimethyltryptamine), psilocin and psilocybin, DOM (dimethoxy methylamphetamine, also called STP), THC (tetrahydrocannabinol, the active ingredient in marijuana), MDA (methylenedioxyamphetamine), some general anesthetics, such as ether and nitrous oxide (laughing gas), and a few others.

Because hallucinogens differ widely in chemical structure, some experts have suggested that the term psychedelic — which is the more exact term used to describe drugs that distort perception rather than those that simply stimulate hallucinations — is a better classification for certain drugs. Consequently, psychedelic drugs are similar in that each alters sensory perception by duplicating the effect of the neurotransmitter serotonin.

Other drugs can precipitate hallucinations and are psychotomimetic (can cause psychosis), but they — unlike psychedelics — affect different neurotransmitters and produce hallucinogenic effects instead of altering or distorting perception. In the late 1960s, for example, drugs that inhibit the neurotransmitter acetylcholine became popular within the drug culture. *Belladonna*, atropine, and scopolamine, to name a few of the better-known ones, increase heart rate, euphoria, and dreamless sleep. And drugs that mimic acetylcholine cause intoxication, hallucinations, delirium, and stupor followed by excitement and auditory and visual hallucinations. Cocaine, amphetamine, and depressants also have certain effects that are marginally similar to those produced by psychedelic drugs. Nevertheless, all these drugs are fundamentally different from psychedelic drugs because they are characterized by how they impair mental processes or dull the senses.

Psychedelic drugs, on the other hand, alter perception and — in effect — make people hyperalert and attuned to a different "reality." They work by mimicking serotonin, a neurotransmitter that plays a significant role in brain communication. By duplicating the effects of serotonin — which regulates emotions, sensory perception, and sleep — such psychedelics as LSD, DOM, DMT, mescaline, MDA, MDMA (methylenedioxy-N-methylamphetamine, known as Ecstasy on the

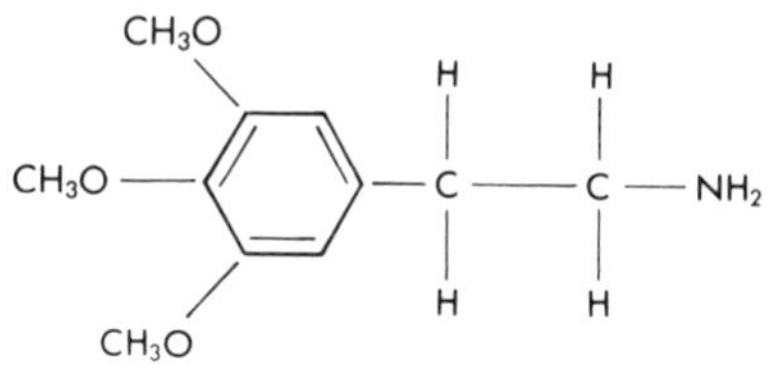

mescaline

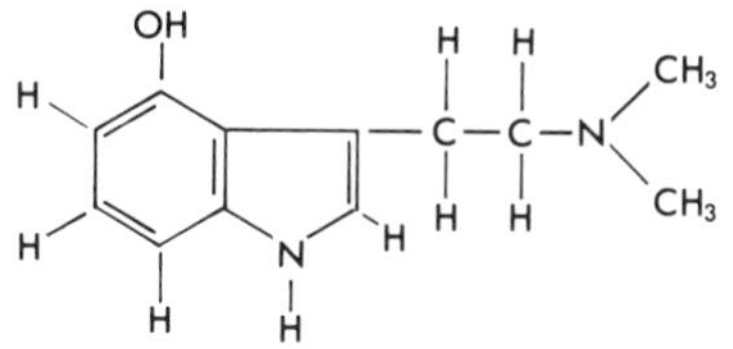

psilocin

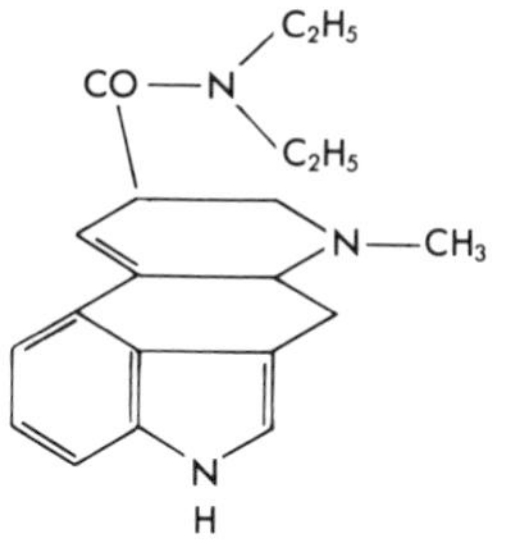

lysergic acid diethylamide (LSD)

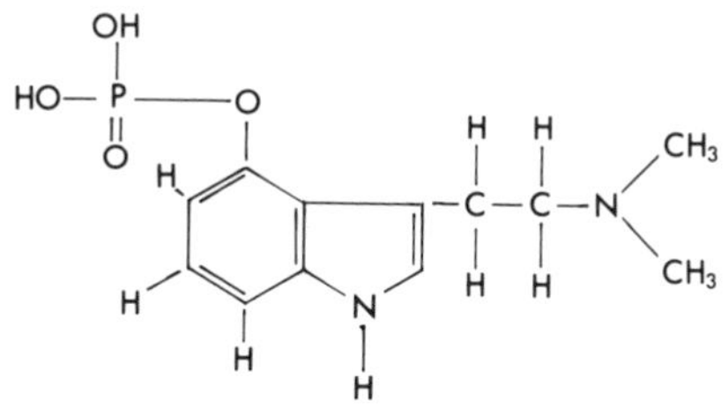

psilocybin

Psychedelic drugs such as psilocin, psilocybin, LSD, and mescaline are similar in that each alters sensory perception by duplicating the effect of the neurotransmitter serotonin.

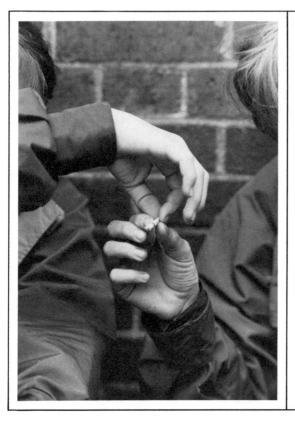

Some researchers suggest that long-term use of THC, the psychoactive ingredient in marijuana, may decrease motivation, performance, and memory.

street), psilocybin, and psilocin have a profound effect on the mind. In effect, the drugs alter brain communication by slowing the activity of neurons responsible for regulating emotion.

These chemical actions and reactions are very complex, as is the influence of these drugs on behavior, sensation, and motor function. To say the drugs are used purely for recreational purposes is to misunderstand the hallucinogenic drug experience and oversimplify the reasons people take them. Some do use these drugs to get high, but there are others who see their use as mystical and use them as a vehicle for expanding consciousness. That they do so at some significant peril goes without saying. And although people talk of enjoying psychedelic experiences, many also use such words as "enlightening," "interesting," "unpleasant," and even "terrifying" to describe the experience.

One of the best descriptions of both the pleasant and unpleasant effects of psychedelic drug action comes from Albert Hofmann himself after he accidentally came under the influence of LSD for the first time:

> I was seized by a peculiar sensation of vertigo and restlessness. Objects, as well as the shapes of my associates in the laboratory, appeared to undergo optical changes. I was unable to concentrate on my work. In a dreamlike state I left for home, where an irresistible urge to lie down came over me. I drew the curtains and immediately fell into a peculiar state similar to drunkenness, characterized by an exaggerated imagination. With my eyes closed, fantastic pictures of extraordinary plasticity and intensive color seemed to surge toward me. After two hours this state gradually wore off.

Hofmann also experienced the first LSD-influenced bad trip, when he inadvertently took a massive dose of his own discovery.

> After 40 minutes I noted the following symptoms in my laboratory journal: slight giddiness, restlessness, difficulty in concentration, visual disturbances, laughing.... Later I lost all count of time. I noticed with dismay that my environment was undergoing progressive changes. My visual field wavered and everything appeared deformed as in a faulty mirror. Space and time became more and more disorganized and I was overcome by a fear that I was going out of my mind. The worst part of it being that I was clearly aware of my condition.
>
> ... Occasionally, I felt as if I were out of my body. I thought I had died. My ego seemed suspended somewhere in space, from where I saw my dead body lying on the sofa.

Marijuana

Aside from compounds that have identified effects on neuroreceptors, other psychedelic drugs are more difficult to classify in terms of which neurotransmitters and neuroreceptors are involved.

A police team experiments with a "human net" used to restrain people who have become violent while under the influence of PCP, a drug that can trigger manic and sometimes psychotic behavior.

Marijuana, for example, an intoxicating plant from which the drug THC (the active ingredient) is derived, could fit in any number of categories. Because marijuana has calming effects when taken in low to moderate doses, experts could easily classify the drug as a mild sedative/hypnotic; however, unlike the sedative/ hypnotics, high doses do not produce coma or death. Although researchers have been unable to determine what sites in the brain THC affects, they point to its ability to alter perception especially when large doses of the drug are present in the body — as reason enough to characterize marijuana as a mild psychedelic drug.

Marijuana often relaxes people who smoke or ingest small amounts of the drug, but it can also have some fairly disturbing side effects at higher doses. Moreover, because it is stored in the body for long periods, even small doses have a cumulative effect — enough to precipitate either very pleasurable or very unpleasant reactions in some people. At high doses, the drug usually produces euphoria, hallucinations, and heightened awareness. It also can produce acute anxiety attacks, acute psychotic reactions, and paranoia. And some researchers suggest that long-term use of THC may decrease motivation, performance, and memory.

Psychedelic Anesthetics

The hallucinogens/psychedelics also include certain drugs that were initially developed as animal anesthetics but were found to cause intense reactions — including insanity — in humans. PCP (phencyclidine), which has powerful hallucinogenic effects, is probably the best known drug in this group. To date, researchers have not been able to trace PCP action to any specific neuroreceptor site or identify the specific neurotransmitter the drug modifies or mimics.

Use of PCP is particularly dangerous because it can produce psychotic reactions in addition to manic behavior, floating sensations, and physical and emotional numbness. In high doses, the drug can produce stupor, coma, and death. Experts suggest that many of the horror stories associated with LSD and other hallucinogens should probably be attributed to PCP. Unfortunately, PCP is often sold under false pretenses as LSD, mescaline, THC, or similar, and less dangerous, hallucinogens. The results are often tragic. A single dose of PCP can cause psychosis, and PCP-induced psychosis can last for months.

Initially, 19th-century researchers used psychedelics — primarily cannabis (marijuana) and mescaline as models for psychosis. (That is, researchers believed that the behavior of people who had taken these drugs could be used as a model for scientists studying psychotic behavior.) The practice lasted into the 1950s, when it was finally abandoned because it showed little promise as a tool for curing major mental illness. Recently, however, researchers have begun to look seriously at the effects of PCP as a potential model for psychosis.

An addict lights an opium pipe. The oldest of the narcotic drugs, opium has been used for its medicinal properties — and abused for its psychoactive ones — for more than 5,000 years.

CHAPTER 5

NARCOTICS

Narcotics. The word has a sinister ring to it. It brings to mind a slew of stereotypes: the junkie, looking for another heroin fix; the world of organized crime, complete with low-life hoodlums and their overlord bosses; the undercover police detective looking for the big bust. Add the word opiates — another term used to classify these drugs — and the scenario becomes even more sinister: opium dens, smugglers, ancient corruption—all come readily to mind.

It is no mistake that these stereotypes abound. The fact is, narcotics were among the first drugs that people ever used and abused. The use of opium, which is extracted from the seeds of the opium poppy, dates back to 4000 B.C.E. (Before the Common Era, the same period as B.C.) when it was used in ancient Mesopotamia for its medicinal properties. The ancient Greeks, who bought and sold opium cakes on the streets of their towns and cities, were probably the first to use narcotics regularly for recreational purposes. Even Homer, the author of the ancient Greek epic masterpieces the *Iliad* and the *Odyssey*, wrote about opium's sedating effects.

The 19th century saw narcotics become the drugs of choice for certain segments of the literary set. A case in point is Thomas De Quincey, who in the early 1800s outlined both

A heroin addict openly prepares his "fix" in this 1920 scene. Ironically, heroin was initially hailed as a nonaddictive alternative to morphine.

the ecstasies and the nightmares of narcotic addiction in his book *Confessions of an English Opium Eater*. Samuel Taylor Coleridge wrote part of his famous epic poem "Kubla Khan" while under the influence of opium. As for the opiates themselves, Coleridge sang their praises when he wrote: "Laudanum gave me repose, not sleep; but you, I believe, know how divine that repose is, what a spot of enchantment, a green spot of fountains and flowers and trees in the very heart of a waste."

The Rise of Addiction

In 1803, Frederick Serteurner, a German scientist, added to the history of opiates when he was able to isolate a concentrated narcotic compound from the opium poppy. The compound was so powerful that a small amount produced astonishing effects. This chemical, which Serteurner called morphine (after Morpheus, the Greek god of dreams), was highly touted for its therapeutic properties; indeed, it changed the nature of medical treatment forever. Unfortunately, it also added to the number of people addicted to opium.

Ignorance was much to blame for this rise in addiction. People simply were not aware of how dangerous these seemingly benign compounds were. The British, for example, reacted to reports of opium's adverse effects in China by concluding that the Chinese were somehow susceptible to the drug while Western people were not. Then, in 1853 the Scottish physician Alexander Wood invented the hypodermic syringe, and word went out that injecting morphine might be a way of avoiding addiction. Couple that misconception with the synthesis of heroin — which physicians and manufacturers doled out as a supposedly nonaddicting cough medicine—and the results were disastrous.

The opium poppy is a major crop for farmers in regions of Southeast Asia. This poppy seed pod, fairly bursting with raw opium, will be split by a harvester collecting its potent and psychoactive juices.

By 1900 the ranks of the addicted in America alone swelled to an estimated one to four million. The tragedy was that many of those people first became addicted because they treated their very legitimate illnesses with patent medicines that just so happened to contain such narcotics as heroin, morphine, or opium. Still, for all the millions of addicts, there was little social stigma attached to narcotics use. Respectable people used narcotics socially, and temperance groups — organizations that sought and for a brief time achieved the prohibition of alcohol in the United States — paid little attention to the growing number of opiate addicts. In fact, some physicians of the time even credited morphine and opium

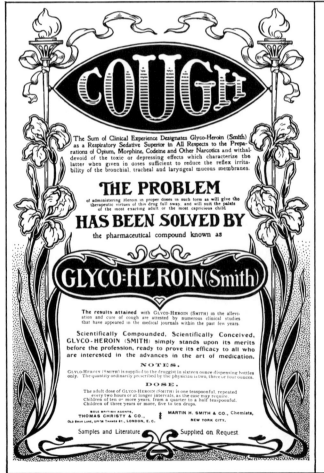

A 1903 advertisement for a cough medication laced with heroin. At the turn of the century, many patent medicines contained opium derivatives, and the ranks of the addicted in America alone swelled to an estimated 4 million.

with the ability to increase people's intellectual ability and, in the words of one, "to make the individual, for a time, a better and greater man."

The Double-edged Sword

As their history would indicate, narcotics are powerful compounds that have served both good and destructive causes. On the one hand, they have been essential to the medical world. On the other, they are strong, addictive agents that people have turned to for relief and pleasure — often with tragic results — for thousands of years. For many, narcotics have led to the worst possible bad trips: addiction and death.

Acting primarily on the central nervous system, the eyes, and the gastrointestinal tract, these drugs produce a host of different effects that run the gamut from pain to pleasure. From drowsiness and mental confusion to euphoria, from nausea and vomiting to peace of mind, from a general sense of well-being to addiction and death, the effects of these drugs are truly complex.

Experts believe the drugs work by interacting with enkephalin neuroreceptors, which, as we have said, are the brain's receptors for natural opiate substances. If this is, in fact, the case, it explains the great ability narcotics have to control pain. Recent studies further underscore that notion, suggesting that the enkephalins and opiate receptor sites play a significant role in the pain-relieving effects of anesthetics and acupuncture. As for death from narcotic overdose, the effects of these drugs on the body's respiratory system are responsible. In small doses, narcotics slow respiration; in larger doses, they can stop a person's ability to breathe altogether.

"The Baddest Trip of All"

But, of course, it was the pleasurable aspects of the opiates that paved the way to addiction, which is, for many people, worse than death. Because the effects of the opiates are so pleasurable, their use almost always leads to addiction, which some call the "baddest trip of all."

Consider the insidious way heroin took hold of the late saxophonist Art Pepper. Here he describes his initial experience with heroin:

I felt this peace like a kind of warmth. I could feel it start in my stomach. From the whole inside of my body I felt the tranquility. It was so relaxing. It was so gorgeous. Sheila said, "Look at yourself in the mirror! Look in the mirror!" And that's what I'd always done: I'd stood and looked at myself in the mirror and I'd talk to myself and say how rotten I was—"Why do people hate you? Why are you alone? Why are you so miserable?" I thought, "Oh, no! I don't want to do that! I don't want to spoil this feeling that's coming up in me!" I was afraid that if I looked in the mirror I would see it, my whole past life, and this wonderful feeling would end, but she kept saying, "Look at yourself! Look how beautiful you are!". . . I looked in the mirror and I looked like an angel. I looked at my pupils and they were pinpoints; they were tiny little dots. It was like looking into a whole universe of joy and happiness and contentment.

. . . I loved myself, everything about myself. I loved my talent. I had lost the sour taste of the filthy alcohol that made me vomit and the feelings of the bennies [Benzedrine, a stimulant] and the strips that put chills up and down my spine. I looked at myself and I looked at Sheila and I looked at the few remaining lines of heroin and I took the dollar bill and horned [inhaled] the rest of them down. I said, "This is it. This is the only answer for me. If this is what it takes, then this is what I'm going to do, whatever dues I have to pay."

. . . I realized from that moment on I would be, if you want to use the word, a junkie. That's the word they used. That's the word they still use. That is what I became at that moment. That's what I practiced; and that's what I still am. And that's what I will die as—a junkie.

For all the euphoria in Pepper's recollection, the ultimate message is one of imprisonment, inferiority, and self-destruction. His was a life of desperation. Pepper was not alone in his plight. Consider the description of addiction written by William Burroughs, himself a heroin addict, in the introduction of his famous book *Naked Lunch*:

I lived in one room in the Native Quarter of Tangier. I had not taken a bath in a year nor changed my clothes or removed them except to stick a needle

every hour in the fibrous grey wooden flesh of
terminal addiction. . . . I was only roused to action
when the hourglass of junk ran out. If a friend came
to visit—and they rarely did since who or what was
left to visit—I sat there. . . . If he had died on the spot,
I would have sat there looking at my shoe waiting to
go through his pockets. Wouldn't you? Because I
never had enough junk—no one ever does.

The scourge of heroin addiction continues to plague
society in the 1980s, despite various legal, medical, and ed-
ucational campaigns to stamp it out. Many law-enforcement
officials and health-care professionals acknowledge that the
problem is unmanageable. They simply do not have the resources to eradicate narcotics addiction, they say. It is a frightening predicament, especially when police officials and
sociologists point to heroin addiction as the single most significant factor in the spread of crime. The culprit, of course,
is the never-ending need junkies have for more money to
buy more drugs.

The death of basketball star Len Bias in 1986 forced the public to reexamine its love affair with cocaine. Reportedly, Bias suffered cardiac arrest when this drug radically increased his heart rate.

CHAPTER 6

SEDATIVES AND STIMULANTS

From the earliest days of recorded history, people have used drugs to relieve anxiety, to induce sleep, and to escape from pressures by getting drunk or "stoned." In almost every instance, the drug in question was no doubt a depressant or "downer" — the name these compounds go by in the drug culture.

In most instances, people have turned to depressants for their medicinal properties — from the calming effects of certain herbs to the sedative action of alcohol. In the Middle Ages, for example, alcohol — by far the most used and abused of the depressant drugs — was considered the elixir of life, and even in the 1980s it is sometimes prescribed in small doses as a minor tranquilizer. In addition to alcohol, the larger family of depressant compounds has played a significant role in alleviating misery for thousands of years.

Classifying the Sedative/Hypnotics

Medically known as sedatives and hypnotic drugs, these compounds run the gamut of chemical structures. To varying degrees they produce depressed behavior. That is, they can produce anything from a mild calming effect to severe depression of the central nervous system — up to, and including, death.

Shizechizo Izumi, 117 years old when this picture was taken, attributes his longevity to sugar-cane liquor. Indeed, some studies show that moderate drinking can prolong life by reducing stress.

As a rule, sedative-hypnotic drugs are divided into four groups: barbiturates, nonbarbiturate hypnotics, antianxiety agents, and miscellaneous drugs that differ in chemical structure from those in the other three groups but produce much the same effect and act in much the same manner. In addition, drugs in any of these four groups can be further classified as anesthetics, hypnotics, sedatives, or tranquilizers.

The modern history of these compounds dates to Joseph Priestley's discovery of nitrous oxide (laughing gas) in 1772 — a drug that is still used widely as an anesthetic. More recent history centers on barbiturates, which date to 1864 when barbituric acid was first prepared. It was, however, not until 1903 that the first barbiturate derivative — barbital — was synthesized. That was followed in 1912 by the introduction of phenobarbital — one of the most widely prescribed barbiturates — which pharmacists initially sold under the trade name Luminal.

Doctors primarily prescribed these drugs to treat the twin plagues of insomnia and anxiety. In the early days, before barbiturates and other antianxiety agents were available, physicians generally relied on alcohol and such opiates as laudanum (a combination of opium and alcohol) to treat these conditions. But the danger was always there: Addiction was far too often the result. And true to the dangers associated with those strong drugs, alcoholism and addiction to laudanum and other opiates came to be a societal curse in the 18th and 19th centuries — a situation that is not all that unfamiliar today.

So, when scientists first synthesized barbiturates, physicians were very pleased. Tested on animals and humans, barbital produced the same desired effect as alcohol and opiates, but apparently without the dangers associated with the supposedly more addictive, older drugs. Instead of prescribing wine in the mid-morning and afternoon to relieve anxiety, and a nightcap at bedtime to induce sleep, physicians were able to treat patients with small doses of barbiturate for anx-

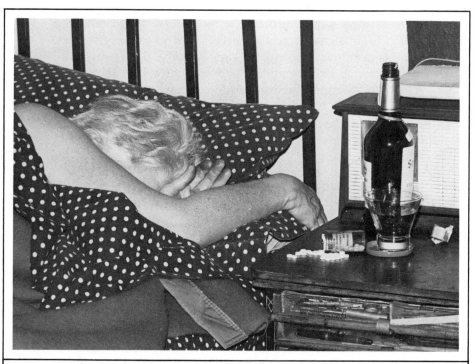

A dramatization of an alcohol and barbiturate overdose. This is a potentially deadly combination, because both of these substances act as central nervous system depressants.

iety and larger doses for insomnia. Barbital — manufactured under the trade name Veronal in 1903 — soon became extremely popular.

But what the early 20th-century scientists did not know is that sedative/hypnotics are very potent drugs that produce a wide range of effects — including very dangerous ones when abused. These drugs include tranquilizers to reduce anxiety, barbiturates to induce sleep or sedation, and analgesics and anesthetics to relieve pain, but they can also cause addiction, coma, and death. When two or more of these drugs are combined, the effect is magnified; many accidental deaths are attributed to this kind of drug mixing.

How the Depressants Work

Also known as general depressants, barbiturates and other sedative-hypnotic drugs work by *depressing* the activity of brain, nerve, and muscle tissue. The drugs accomplish this by inhibiting communication between the synapses along which brain signals travel. As mentioned in earlier chapters, neurotransmitters carry these signals from cell to cell; in the meantime, as also mentioned earlier, certain drugs inhibit, stimulate, or mimic neurotransmitters and thus have significant effects on brain communication. In the case of general depressants, the drugs inhibit and slow brain communication by enhancing the effect of GABA, the brain's major inhibiting neurotransmitter.

In the case of severe anxiety, the inhibiting effect of a depressant is just what the doctor ordered. But in the case of a healthy person whose brain chemistry is normal, depressants can seriously slow and impair behavior.

Classifying the Stimulants

The central stimulants are drugs that increase body activity. From behavioral activity to thought processes to mood elevation, the actions of these compounds are characterized by rapidity. The individual drugs in this category, however, differ significantly when it comes to their molecular structure. Consequently, these compounds cannot be classified as easily as depressants. Instead, central stimulants are subdivided into several groups that share similar characteristics based on how they act.

Stimulants work by increasing the action of norepineph-rine, a neurotransmitter (mentioned in earlier chapters) that affects anxiety and stimulates the central nervous system. Consequently, these drugs elevate mood and increase activity in any person who takes them. Drugs in this category are often prescribed as "diet drugs" or appetite suppressants and — in some instances — to control hyperactive behavior. (This may seem paradoxical, but stimulants somehow do control hyperactivity in children.) Best known among these drugs are cocaine and the amphetamines. Other drugs in this cat-egory include diethylpropion (brand names: Tenuate, Te-panil), methylphenidate (Ritalin), and phenmetrazine (Preludin).

A second group of stimulants includes several drugs that cause convulsions, such as strychnine (a commonly used rat poison), which is sometimes used to "cut" (adulterate) LSD because of its ability to mimic some of the effects of hallu-cinogens when taken in minuscule doses.

These proper ladies and gentlemen would no doubt have been shocked to learn that the coffee they are drinking contains a drug — caffeine — with side effects ranging from the jitters to dependence.

Caffeine and Nicotine

The third group contains the most commonly used — and abused — central stimulants: caffeine and nicotine. In the case of caffeine, body activity is stimulated when the drug increases cell metabolism within nerve cells. Nicotine, on the other hand, works by stimulating certain cells within the brain and in the nervous system.

Both these drugs have their downside.

Even caffeine, which until recent years was considered harmless, can have serious side effects, including dependence. Caffeine withdrawal, among people who drink many cups of coffee or soft drinks with high levels of caffeine each day, is often accompanied by shaking and tremors, sleep distur-

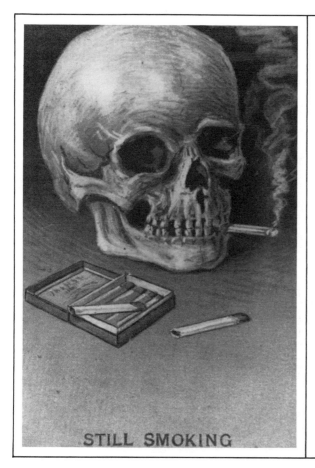

STILL SMOKING

Although the dangers of cigarette smoking are well documented, nicotine is so addictive that many smokers who wish to quit are unable to do so.

bances, irritability, and headaches. And if anyone doubts the popularity of caffeine, he or she need only consider the amount consumed each year in the United States: approximately 15 million pounds. The abuse of caffeine, a powerful stimulant of nerve tissue in the brain, is nothing to laugh about. The drug's side effects can be quite serious. Insomnia, agitation, increased heart rate and occasional arrhythmias (abnormal and sometimes dangerous fluctuations in heart rate), and even mild delirium are among the effects of too much caffeine.

Nicotine, of course, is one of the most addictive drugs available, and withdrawal from its effects is serious business. In addition to all the withdrawal symptoms that accompany caffeine withdrawal, nicotine withdrawal is usually marked by a craving for the drug. Nicotine produces a powerful effect on the brain, the spinal cord, the peripheral nervous system, the heart, the lungs, and various other parts of the body. It stimulates the central nervous system at every level, and can produce irritability and tremors, intestinal cramps, diarrhea, increased heart rate and blood pressure, and dizziness. But by far the worst effect of nicotine is on the heart. Experts have written volumes on the effect of smoking — the most common way nicotine is ingested. The numbers are staggering: 362,000 people die each year from tobacco use. Of those deaths, 62,000 are from lung disease; 130,000 from cancer; and 170,000 from heart and vascular disease. The most telling statistic of all: Each cigarette a person smokes reduces his or her life by 14 minutes.

Amphetamines

In recent years, cocaine and amphetamines (commonly called "speed" on the street) have taken center stage when it comes to abuse of central stimulants.

The drug amphetamine, first synthesized in 1887, saw its first medical use in the 1930s, when researchers discovered that it increases blood pressure, stimulates the central nervous system, and dilates the nasal and bronchial passages (which is especially helpful in the treatment of asthma). The drug was subsequently manufactured and sold under the trade name Benzedrine. Since then, a host of new amphetamines has been synthesized. From Benzedrine to Dexedrine to methamphetamine, the drugs are powerful and can be very dangerous. On the street they go by a number of different names: speed, crystal, glass, meth—to name but a few.

When they were first synthesized, amphetamines were highly acclaimed. Used to promote alert behavior, to stave off unwanted drowsiness, and to lift depression, amphetamines were considered beneficial tonics. In time, however, the dangerous side effects — the bad trips — became all too well known. In larger doses, for example, researchers found that amphetamines cause depression, agitation, and fatigue. They noted other serious effects, too, including headaches, palpitations, dizziness, apprehension, delirium, and — with time—addiction.

As mentioned in earlier chapters, serious amphetamine abuse leads to very dangerous consequences. Prolonged use of high doses of the drugs often results in psychosis or other abnormal mental conditions, weight loss, skin sores, apathy, and infections caused by neglect of personal hygiene. These serious side effects have prompted people to label amphetamine use as a real killer. Although the drug — even in very high doses — rarely causes death when it is the only drug taken, it kills in other ways. In the 1960s, people labeled amphetamines "speed" because of the rush of adrenaline and activity they produce. They also recognized that its effects could be destructive — even deadly. It can snuff out spirit, motivation, and mental health. Long-term abuse can lead to irreparable psychosis caused by drug-induced organic brain damage.

By far the worst form of amphetamine abuse is intravenous (injected directly into the blood) use. Called "mainlining" on the street, intravenous use is particularly insidious. Dr. John C. Kramer, writing in the *Journal of the American Medical Association* in 1967, noted how mainlining was becoming dangerously popular. "The experience somehow differs from the effects of oral amphetamines not only quantitatively but also qualitatively. [It is for the first-time user] an ecstatic experience, [causing him or her to think] 'Where has this been all my life?' "

Compare that initial ecstasy, however, with the psychotic reaction of a long-term amphetamine abuser who took 150 mg of the "diet drug," Tenuate Dospan:

Want to fight back, or stare back: sour stomach, straw feeling, head full of cotton, can't breath very well, all stiff around the ribs. Feel like a mannequin — joints don't move easily; stiff, jerky movements. Move: go into different plane. Stopped from participating in life (people, newspaper-reading, studying anthropology) by dizzying feeling, emotional dizziness, of "too much." My head becomes light — change from drab to vital is too much — punishment will follow. Open up dark, secret corners of life (against Mom) — too much (unwholesome) intensity of emotion, like some kind of psyched-up violin playing — not words (I'm not human after all) leads to screwed-up emotions, as a punishment — like Faust opening Pandora's little box. (Afraid, head spins.) Terrible doom as a result of expanding imagination.

Cocaine

Unlike amphetamine, which is a relatively new drug, cocaine has a long history. The Spanish *conquistadores* first encountered the active use of cocaine in its unrefined state when they found the highly advanced Inca civilization in the early 16th century. The emperor of the Incas, as well as priests and supplicants were allowed to chew the leaves of the shrub *erythroxylon coca* and enjoy the euphoria the plant produces. (Cocaine is derived from erythroxylon coca and is far more powerful in its effects than the leaves alone.) The Spanish never took to the drug themselves. They did, however, use it to enslave the Incas, doling it out to reward and to increase productivity.

Over the centuries the drug evolved to the point that its use was seen as a sign of sophistication. Cocaine was derived from the coca leaf and used in plenty of situations. In the late 19th century, for example, Coca-Cola was bottled with a dash of cocaine in it. In the 1930s Cole Porter, in one of his hit songs, wrote: "I get no kick from cocaine ... [but] I get a kick out of you." The suggestion, of course, was that cocaine was certainly giving plenty of people a kick — enough so that it was perfectly respectable to mention it, albeit somewhat naughtily, in a song.

These days, newspapers, television, magazines, and books have had plenty to say about cocaine abuse. For a while

Bolivian farmers selling their harvest of coca leaves at an open market. Much of these crops are bought by middlemen, who process the leaves into cocaine, which is then sold for enormous profit.

it was — and to some degree still is — the drug of choice among the upwardly mobile and supposedly glamorous sets. Like the ancient Incas, however, many people are learning that the aura of glamour and privilege that surrounds cocaine abuse is outweighed by the drug's ability to enslave those who use it. Unfortunately, there are still those who think it is worth taking — if only to increase short-term productivity by helping them work harder and longer.

Cocaine's allure is the strong sense of euphoria that it produces. People who take cocaine suddenly have great confidence in their abilities. They feel strong, good-looking, smart, witty, vivacious. They feel nothing is beyond them. But for all the sense of power that cocaine — or "coke," as it is popularly known — gives its user, the feeling is ephemeral and often followed by depression.

In effect, cocaine resembles amphetamine more than any other drug; however, its effect is short-lived. Whereas amphetamines, such as Benzedrine and Dexedrine, might last for several hours, a usual dose of cocaine lasts about a half hour. An especially potent form of cocaine known as "crack" produces a high that lasts only for minutes but is described as so powerful that it is highly addictive. Crack has a more potent effect than cocaine primarily because it is smoked and consequently ingested directly into the bloodstream through the lungs, producing a greatly intensified "rush."

In contrast to the good feelings cocaine produces are the nightmares that prolonged use brings. Increasing dependence, addiction, and even cocaine psychosis (which closely resembles paranoid schizophrenia) often occur — especially in people with addictive personalities. At its worst, cocaine kills — a truth brought home to many by the cocaine-induced deaths of actor-comedian John Belushi, University of Maryland basketball star Len Bias, and an alarmingly large number of others.

Interviewed by *Time* magazine in 1986, Ken — a 33-year-old construction worker from the east side of Cleveland, who

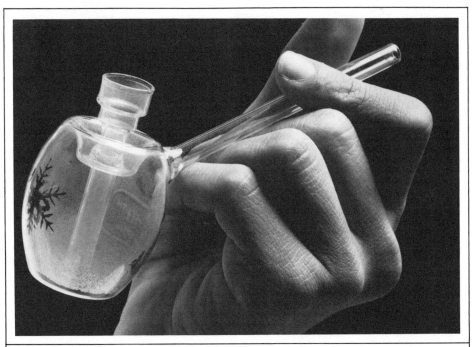

Most "crack" addicts smoke the drug through a pipe for rapid absorption into the bloodstream. This produces a brief, but powerful, high that leaves the user immediately craving more of the drug.

In 1984 comedian John Belushi died of an overdose of heroin and cocaine. Ultimately, the euphoric highs promised by drugs are followed by excruciating lows and, in some cases, even death.

began snorting cocaine with his wife in 1982 — put it well. Cocaine ruined his life, he said. It snuck into his day-to-day affairs, and pretty soon he was blowing his entire paycheck to pay for cocaine. He even began beating his wife. Then, when he tried to quit, his wife, who had become addicted as well, accused him of ruining their relationship by giving up cocaine.

"You don't even see it coming," he said. "We didn't think we were addicted. But once you get into it, it's got you. You don't even have a choice. I became a workaholic, a superman, staying up four or five days at a time."

Conclusion

Until the 20th century — and especially the last two decades — psychoactive drugs were used, but their highly complex nature was not understood. In many ways, they are peculiarly modern, even if they mimic or act on chemical processes as old as the human race itself. Science has learned much about how the human mind works, and in its enlightenment has produced extraordinary drugs that hold the promise of great advances in the treatment of major psychiatric disorders. The other side of that coin is just as significant: The drugs that modern science has either refined or produced include compounds that have enslaved millions of people through addiction, stimulated tragic psychological consequences, and resulted in uncounted deaths. Drugs are indeed a mixed blessing for society.

For all the good they do, there is also the havoc they wreak. As this book has shown, drugs produce adverse reactions — bad trips — that are as complex and different as the powerful drugs that precipitate them.

APPENDIX

State Agencies
for the Prevention and Treatment
of Drug Abuse

ALABAMA
Department of Mental Health
Division of Mental Illness and
  Substance Abuse Community
  Programs
200 Interstate Park Drive
P.O. Box 3710
Montgomery, AL 36193
(205) 271-9253

ALASKA
Department of Health and Social
  Services
Office of Alcoholism and Drug
  Abuse
Pouch H-05-F
Juneau, AK 99811
(907) 586-6201

ARIZONA
Department of Health Services
Division of Behavioral Health
  Services
Bureau of Community Services
Alcohol Abuse and Alcoholism
  Section
2500 East Van Buren
Phoenix, AZ 85008
(602) 255-1238

Department of Health Services
Division of Behavioral Health
  Services
Bureau of Community Services
Drug Abuse Section
2500 East Van Buren
Phoenix, AZ 85008
(602) 255-1240

ARKANSAS
Department of Human Services
Office of Alcohol and Drug Abuse
  Prevention
1515 West 7th Avenue
Suite 310
Little Rock, AR 72202
(501) 371-2603

CALIFORNIA
Department of Alcohol and Drug
  Abuse
111 Capitol Mall
Sacramento, CA 95814
(916) 445-1940

COLORADO
Department of Health
Alcohol and Drug Abuse Division
4210 East 11th Avenue
Denver, CO 80220
(303) 320-6137

CONNECTICUT
Alcohol and Drug Abuse
  Commission
999 Asylum Avenue
3rd Floor
Hartford, CT 06105
(203) 566-4145

DELAWARE
Division of Mental Health
Bureau of Alcoholism and Drug
  Abuse
1901 North Dupont Highway
Newcastle, DE 19720
(302) 421-6101

DISTRICT OF COLUMBIA
Department of Human Services
Office of Health Planning and
  Development
601 Indiana Avenue, NW
Suite 500
Washington, D.C. 20004
(202) 724-5641

FLORIDA
Department of Health and
  Rehabilitative Services
Alcoholic Rehabilitation Program
1317 Winewood Boulevard
Room 187A
Tallahassee, FL 32301
(904) 488-0396

Department of Health and
  Rehabilitative Services
Drug Abuse Program
1317 Winewood Boulevard
Building 6, Room 155
Tallahassee, FL 32301
(904) 488-0900

GEORGIA
Department of Human Resources
Division of Mental Health and
  Mental Retardation
Alcohol and Drug Section
618 Ponce De Leon Avenue, NE
Atlanta, GA 30365-2101
(404) 894-4785

HAWAII
Department of Health
Mental Health Division
Alcohol and Drug Abuse Branch
1250 Punch Bowl Street
P.O. Box 3378
Honolulu, HI 96801
(808) 548-4280

IDAHO
Department of Health and Welfare
Bureau of Preventive Medicine
Substance Abuse Section
450 West State
Boise, ID 83720
(208) 334-4368

ILLINOIS
Department of Mental Health and
  Developmental Disabilities
Division of Alcoholism
160 North La Salle Street
Room 1500
Chicago, IL 60601
(312) 793-2907

Illinois Dangerous Drugs
  Commission
300 North State Street
Suite 1500
Chicago, IL 60610
(312) 822-9860

INDIANA
Department of Mental Health
Division of Addiction Services
429 North Pennsylvania Street
Indianapolis, IN 46204
(317) 232-7816

IOWA
Department of Substance Abuse
505 5th Avenue
Insurance Exchange Building
Suite 202
Des Moines, IA 50319
(515) 281-3641

KANSAS
Department of Social Rehabilitation
Alcohol and Drug Abuse Services
2700 West 6th Street
Biddle Building
Topeka, KS 66606
(913) 296-3925

KENTUCKY
Cabinet for Human Resources
Department of Health Services
Substance Abuse Branch
275 East Main Street
Frankfort, KY 40601
(502) 564-2880

LOUISIANA
Department of Health and Human
    Resources
Office of Mental Health and
    Substance Abuse
655 North 5th Street
P.O. Box 4049
Baton Rouge, LA 70821
(504) 342-2565

MAINE
Department of Human Services
Office of Alcoholism and Drug
    Abuse Prevention
Bureau of Rehabilitation
32 Winthrop Street
Augusta, ME 04330
(207) 289-2781

MARYLAND
Alcoholism Control Administration
201 West Preston Street
Fourth Floor
Baltimore, MD 21201
(301) 383-2977

State Health Department
Drug Abuse Administration
201 West Preston Street
Baltimore, MD 21201
(301) 383-3312

MASSACHUSETTS
Department of Public Health
Division of Alcoholism
755 Boylston Street
Sixth Floor
Boston, MA 02116
(617) 727-1960

Department of Public Health
Division of Drug Rehabilitation
600 Washington Street
Boston, MA 02114
(617) 727-8617

MICHIGAN
Department of Public Health
Office of Substance Abuse Services
3500 North Logan Street
P.O. Box 30035
Lansing, MI 48909
(517) 373-8603

MINNESOTA
Department of Public Welfare
Chemical Dependency Program
    Division
Centennial Building
658 Cedar Street
4th Floor
Saint Paul, MN 55155
(612) 296-4614

MISSISSIPPI
Department of Mental Health
Division of Alcohol and Drug Abuse
1102 Robert E. Lee Building
Jackson, MS 39201
(601) 359-1297

MISSOURI
Department of Mental Health
Division of Alcoholism and Drug
    Abuse
2002 Missouri Boulevard
P.O. Box 687
Jefferson City, MO 65102
(314) 751-4942

MONTANA
Department of Institutions
Alcohol and Drug Abuse Division
1539 11th Avenue
Helena, MT 59620
(406) 449-2827

NEBRASKA
Department of Public Institutions
Division of Alcoholism and Drug
Abuse
801 West Van Dorn Street
P.O. Box 94728
Lincoln, NB 68509
(402) 471-2851, Ext. 415

NEVADA
Department of Human Resources
Bureau of Alcohol and Drug Abuse
505 East King Street
Carson City, NV 89710
(702) 885-4790

NEW HAMPSHIRE
Department of Health and Welfare
Office of Alcohol and Drug Abuse
  Prevention
Hazen Drive
Health and Welfare Building
Concord, NH 03301
(603) 271-4627

NEW JERSEY
Department of Health
Division of Alcoholism
129 East Hanover Street CN 362
Trenton, NJ 08625
(609) 292-8949

Department of Health
Division of Narcotic and Drug
  Abuse Control
129 East Hanover Street CN 362
Trenton, NJ 08625
(609) 292-8949

NEW MEXICO
Health and Environment Department
Behavioral Services Division
Substance Abuse Bureau
725 Saint Michaels Drive
P.O. Box 968
Santa Fe, NM 87503
(505) 984-0020, Ext. 304

NEW YORK
Division of Alcoholism and Alcohol
  Abuse
194 Washington Avenue
Albany, NY 12210
(518) 474-5417

Division of Substance Abuse
  Services
Executive Park South
Box 8200
Albany, NY 12203
(518) 457-7629

NORTH CAROLINA
Department of Human Resources
Division of Mental Health, Mental
  Retardation and Substance Abuse
  Services
Alcohol and Drug Abuse Services
325 North Salisbury Street
Albemarle Building
Raleigh, NC 27611
(919) 733-4670

NORTH DAKOTA
Department of Human Services
Division of Alcoholism and Drug
  Abuse
State Capitol Building
Bismarck, ND 58505
(701) 224-2767

OHIO
Department of Health
Division of Alcoholism
246 North High Street
P.O. Box 118
Columbus, OH 43216
(614) 466-3543

Department of Mental Health
Bureau of Drug Abuse
65 South Front Street
Columbus, OH 43215
(614) 466-9023

OKLAHOMA
Department of Mental Health
Alcohol and Drug Programs
4545 North Lincoln Boulevard
Suite 100 East Terrace
P.O. Box 53277
Oklahoma City, OK 73152
(405) 521-0044

OREGON
Department of Human Resources
Mental Health Division
Office of Programs for Alcohol and
   Drug Problems
2575 Bittern Street, NE
Salem, OR 97310
(503) 378-2163

PENNSYLVANIA
Department of Health
Office of Drug and Alcohol
   Programs
Commonwealth and Forster Avenues
Health and Welfare Building
P.O. Box 90
Harrisburg, PA 17108
(717) 787-9857

RHODE ISLAND
Department of Mental Health,
   Mental Retardation and Hospitals
Division of Substance Abuse
Substance Abuse Administration
   Building
Cranston, RI 02920
(401) 464-2091

SOUTH CAROLINA
Commission on Alcohol and Drug
   Abuse
3700 Forest Drive
Columbia, SC 29204
(803) 758-2521

SOUTH DAKOTA
Department of Health
Division of Alcohol and Drug Abuse
523 East Capitol, Joe Foss Building
Pierre, SD 57501
(605) 773-4806

TENNESSEE
Department of Mental Health and
   Mental Retardation
Alcohol and Drug Abuse Services
505 Deaderick Street
James K. Polk Building,
   Fourth Floor
Nashville, TN 37219
(615) 741-1921

TEXAS
Commission on Alcoholism
809 Sam Houston State Office
   Building
Austin, TX 78701
(512) 475-2577
Department of Community Affairs
Drug Abuse Prevention Division
2015 South Interstate Highway 35
P.O. Box 13166
Austin, TX 78711
(512) 443-4100

UTAH
Department of Social Services
Division of Alcoholism and Drugs
150 West North Temple
Suite 350
P.O. Box 2500
Salt Lake City, UT 84110
(801) 533-6532

VERMONT
Agency of Human Services
Department of Social and
   Rehabilitation Services
Alcohol and Drug Abuse Division
103 South Main Street
Waterbury, VT 05676
(802) 241-2170

VIRGINIA
Department of Mental Health and
Mental Retardation
Division of Substance Abuse
109 Governor Street
P.O. Box 1797
Richmond, VA 23214
(804) 786-5313

WASHINGTON
Department of Social and Health
Service
Bureau of Alcohol and Substance
Abuse
Office Building—44 W
Olympia, WA 98504
(206) 753-5866

WEST VIRGINIA
Department of Health
Office of Behavioral Health Services
Division on Alcoholism and Drug
Abuse
1800 Washington Street East
Building 3 Room 451
Charleston, WV 25305
(304) 348-2276

WISCONSIN
Department of Health and Social
Services
Division of Community Services
Bureau of Community Programs
Alcohol and Other Drug Abuse
Program Office
1 West Wilson Street
P.O. Box 7851
Madison, WI 53707
(608) 266-2717

WYOMING
Alcohol and Drug Abuse Programs
Hathaway Building
Cheyenne, WY 82002
(307) 777-7115, Ext. 7118

GUAM
Mental Health & Substance Abuse
Agency
P.O. Box 20999
Guam 96921

PUERTO RICO
Department of Addiction Control
Services
Alcohol Abuse Programs
P.O. Box B-Y Rio Piedras Station
Rio Piedras, PR 00928
(809) 763-5014

Department of Addiction Control
Services
Drug Abuse Programs
P.O. Box B-Y Rio Piedras Station
Rio Piedras, PR 00928
(809) 764-8140

VIRGIN ISLANDS
Division of Mental Health,
Alcoholism & Drug Dependency
Services
P.O. Box 7329
Saint Thomas, Virgin Islands 00801
(809) 774-7265

AMERICAN SAMOA
LBJ Tropical Medical Center
Department of Mental Health Clinic
Pago Pago, American Samoa 96799

TRUST TERRITORIES
Director of Health Services
Office of the High Commissioner
Saipan, Trust Territories 96950

Further Reading

Goodwin, Donald W. *Alcoholism:The Facts*. New York: Oxford University Press, 1981.

Grinspoon, Lester, and James B. Bakalar. *Psychedelic Drugs Reconsidered*. New York: Basic Books, 1979.

Grinspoon, Lester. *The Speed Culture — Amphetamine Use and Abuse in America*. Cambridge, MA: Harvard University Press, 1975.

Kirsch, M.M. *Designer Drugs*. Minneapolis: CompCare Publications, 1986.

Mothner, Ira and Alan Weitz. *How to Get Off Drugs*. New York: Rolling Stone Press/Simon and Schuster, 1984.

Snyder, Solomon H. *Drugs and the Brain*. New York: Scientific American Books, 1986.

Glossary

acetylcholine a neurotransmitter that plays an important part in the transmission of nerve impulses, especially at synapses

addiction a condition caused by repeated drug use, characterized by a compulsive urge to continue using the drug, a tendency to increase the dosage, and physiological and/or psychological dependence

alkaloid a nitrogen-containing compound, produced by plants, that affects body functions. Alkaloids commonly used as drugs include morphine, quinine, atropine, and codeine

amphetamine a drug that stimulates the central nervous system, alleviates fatigue, and produces a feeling of alertness and well-being. Although it has been used for weight control, repeated use of the drug can cause restlessness and insomnia

anesthetic a drug that produces a loss of sensation and consciousness; can be local or general

barbiturates drugs that have a depressing effect on the central nervous system and respiration. They have toxic side effects and, when used excessively, can lead to tolerance, dependence, and even death

Belladonna the deadly nightshade plant, parts of which are used as a narcotic and to dilate the pupils

caffeine a central nervous system stimulant found in coffee, tea, cocoa, various soft drinks, and often in combination with other drugs to enhance their effects

cocaine the primary psychoactive ingredient in the coca plant and a behavioral stimulant

codeine a sedative and pain-relieving agent found in opium and related to, but less potent than, morphine

depressant a drug that depresses the central nervous system; used to help people block out unpleasant thoughts and anxieties and reduce tension

detoxification the process by which an addicted individual is gradually withdrawn from the abused drug, usually under medical supervision and sometimes in conjunction with the administration of other drugs

dimethyltryptamine also known as DMT, a powerful psychedelic drug prepared from the beans of the South American *Piptadenia peregrina* tree

endorphins compounds produced in the brain that help regulate pain and stress and serve as the body's natural opiates

enkephalin a type of endorphin, found in the brain, that acts to block pain; can cause physical dependence and depression of the central nervous system

euphoria a mental high characterized by a sense of well-being

GABA gamma-aminobutyric acid; the brain's major inhibitory neurotransmitter, which reduces the activity of the nerve cells it comes in contact with

glia supporting or connective tissue of the central nervous system

hallucinogen a drug that causes the user to see or hear things that aren't there; LSD, peyote, and ethyl alcohol are examples of hallucinogens

hashish a psychoactive substance made from the dried and pressed flowers and leaves of the hemp plant; it contains a high concentration of THC, the active ingredient in the plant

heroin a semisynthetic opiate produced by a chemical modification of morphine

limbic system a group of structures in the brain that are concerned with human emotions and motivation

LSD lysergic acid diethylamide; a hallucinogen derived from a fungus that grows on rye or from morning glory seeds

marijuana a psychoactive substance with the active ingredient THC, found in the crushed leaves, flowers, and branches of the hemp plant

mescaline a psychedelic drug found in the peyote cactus

morphine an opiate used as a sedative and pain reliever

narcotic originally, a group of drugs producing effects similar to morphine; often used to refer to any substance that sedates, has a depressive effect, and/or causes dependence

neuron the fundamental functional unit of neural tissue

neurotransmitter a chemical released by neurons that transmits nerve impulses across gaps called synapses

nicotine a stimulant found in tobacco that causes dependence in habitual smokers

norepinephrine a neurotransmitter found in the autonomic nervous system

opiate compounds from the milky juice of the poppy plant *Papaver somniferum*, including opium, morphine, codeine, and their derivatives (such as heroin)

PCP also called phencyclidine; an illicit drug used for its stimulating, depressing, and/or hallucinogenic effects

physical dependence adaption of the body to the presence of a drug such that its absence produces withdrawal symptoms

psychedelic drug any drug that alters sensory perception and creates changes in the level of consciousness. Hallucinogens are considered psychedelic drugs

psychological dependence a condition in which the drug user craves a drug to maintain a sense of well-being and feels discomfort when deprived of it

psychosis a severe mental illness in which a person loses touch with reality. Hallucinations may occur and thought processes may be altered

psychotomimetic any drug that causes psychosis

receptor a specialized component of a cell that combines with a chemical substance to alter the function of the cell; for example, nerve-cell receptors combine with neurotransmitters

sedative a drug that produces calmness, relaxation, and sleep; barbiturates are considered sedatives

serotonin a compound thought to act as a neurotransmitter in affecting sleep functions; widely distributed throughout the body, it acts similarly to the histamines in combating inflammation

stimulant any drug that increases brain activity and produces the sensation of greater energy, euphoria, and increased alertness

synthesize creating a chemical compound by combining elements or simpler compounds or by degrading a complex compound; generally refers to a laboratory process

tolerance a decrease of susceptibility to the effects of a drug due to its continued administration, resulting in the user's need to increase the drug dosage to achieve the effects experienced previously

tranquilizer an antianxiety drug that has calming and relaxing effects; Librium and Valium are tranquilizers

withdrawal the physiological and psychological effects of discontinued usage of drugs

PICTURE CREDITS

Index

Mark S. Miller is the Public Affairs manager for Ford Aerospace and Communications Corporation in Washington, D.C. He is also a freelance writer whose work in the medical and scientific field has appeared in *The Boston Globe, The Albany Times Union* and Johns Hopkins' *Keynotes Magazine.*

Solomon H. Snyder, M.D. is Distinguished Service Professor of Neuroscience, Pharmacology and Psychiatry at The Johns Hopkins University School of Medicine. He has served as president of the Society for Neuroscience and in 1978 received the Albert Lasker Award in Medical Research. He has authored *Uses of Marijuana, Madness and the Brain, The Troubled Mind, Biological Aspects of Mental Disorder,* and edited *Perspective in Neuropharmacology: A Tribute to Julius Axelrod.* Professor Snyder was a research associate with Dr. Axelrod at the National Institutes of Health.

Barry L. Jacobs, Ph.D., is currently a professor in the program of neuroscience at Princeton University. Professor Jacobs is author of *Serotonin Neurotransmission and Behavior* and *Hallucinogens: Neurochemical, Behavioral and Clinical Perspectives.* He has written many journal articles in the field of neuroscience and contributed numerous chapters to books on behavior and brain science. He has been a member of several panels of the National Institute of Mental Health.

Joann Ellison Rodgers, M.S. (Columbia), became Deputy Director of Public Affairs and Director of Media Relations for the Johns Hopkins Medical Institutions in Baltimore, Maryland, in 1984 after 18 years as an award-winning science journalist and widely read columnist for the Hearst newspapers.